D1613547

The Blood-Horse

Authoritative Guide to

Breeding Thoroughbreds

BY THE STAFF AND CORRESPONDENTS
OF BLOOD-HORSE PUBLICATIONS

Lexington, Kentucky

Library of Congress Control Number: 2006921616

ISBN-13: 978-1-58150-138-4
ISBN-10: 1-58150-138-2

Printed in China
First Edition: 2006

Distributed to the trade by
National Book Network
4501 Forbes Blvd., Suite 200, Lanham, MD 20706
1.800.462.6420

A Division of
Blood-Horse Publications
Publishers Since 1916

Contents

COVER PHOTOGRAPH BY BARBARA D. LIVINGSTON

Introduction

Breeding Thoroughbreds can be an exciting and highly rewarding venture. Few experiences can compare with watching a homebred horse command top dollar at an auction or win a stakes race — they signify that the years of careful planning and waiting having finally paid off.

Newcomers to the breeding business, though, need to approach the endeavor with eyes wide open. Success is not easy and requires equal amounts of education, business savvy, and good luck. *The Blood-Horse Authoritative Guide to Breeding Thoroughbreds* offers a comprehensive overview of the breeding business and explores the elements that comprise a successful program. Though reading this book can't guarantee profits, it can provide helpful guidelines, trends, and considerations newcomers can follow to increase their likelihood of success.

Investing in breeding stock has been an attractive ownership option since the mid-1990s when bloodstock prices started rising. In 2005 the average price for a broodmare sold at auction reached a record $58,235. At the 2005 November breeding stock sale, the champion race filly Ashado sold for a world-record $9 million.

More than one-quarter of every foal crop is sold at yearling auctions. In 2005, for example, 10,088 yearlings sold for an average of $54,910 and a median of $13,500 — records in all categories. Yet despite robust prices, only about one-quarter of

BARBARA D. LIVINGSTON

The dream for many breeders: reaching the winner's circle with a homebred

ANNE M. EBERHARDT

The mating that produced Ashado paid off on the track and in the sales ring

the yearlings sold at auction make a profit.

Also, not every foal becomes a winner at the track. In fact, of the estimated 37,000 foals born in North America each year, less than half of those that make it to the track win races and only 3 percent (or approximately 1,110) win races at the stakes level.

Despite these odds, newcomers to breeding can put themselves ahead of the game by educating themselves about the business and heeding the advice of people who have flourished as breeders or have studied trends and proclivities in the Thoroughbred breeding industry.

The Blood-Horse Authoritative Guide to Breeding Thoroughbreds provides a blueprint for buying and breeding a mare. Readers will learn how and where to acquire a mare and find suggestions from experts on how to select a stallion. They also will learn the fundamentals of conformation as well as the various pedigree theories. In addition, experts discuss some real-life mating decisions that resulted in successful racehorses. Those success stories include Seattle Slew, Monarchos, and Ashado.

The guide also contains a listing of useful resources, examples of a breeding contract and sales catalog pages, frequently asked questions, and a glossary.

Though countless books have been devoted to theories on pedigree and conformation, *The Blood-Horse Authoritative Guide to Breeding Thoroughbreds* will help readers get a feel for the breeding business, its components and trends, in addition to offering a few valuable insights and caveats from those who have bred some of racing's best Thoroughbreds.

THINGS TO KNOW

Do Your Homework!

- Find a reputable adviser: Ask for references and speak with other clients.
- Learn about the industry: Visit farms during breeding season. Spend time at the sales. Spend a day on a racetrack backside. Subscribe to industry publications.
- Study pedigrees and conformation: Talk with pedigree consultants. Evaluate horses at the sales or the racetrack.

PART I

Obtaining a Mare

Finding the Right Mare

So, you want to get into breeding Thoroughbreds? Right off the bat, two important questions come to mind: How much money do you have to spend? What are you going to do with the offspring? In other words, at what level do you want to get involved and do you want to breed to race or to sell?

Your answer to those two questions will greatly influence the type of mare you buy and where you'll find her. Let's say you have $5,000 to purchase a mare. Don't go to the Keeneland November breeding stock sale, especially during the first week, expecting to buy anything. The final few days of that marathon sale will have a few mares in your price range, but you might have more luck looking elsewhere. Shopping at smaller, regional sales and buying off the racetrack are options that would provide you with a better and wider selection of broodmares or broodmare prospects. Of course, if you have the resources to participate in the higher levels of the sport, then you can broaden your search when looking for a mare, allowing you to pursue higher-quality stock.

Let's examine the types of fillies and mares that you can acquire for breeding purposes.

1) Broodmare prospects: Most any healthy unbred filly is a broodmare prospect. You may hear the phrase "residual value" in connection with a filly. That's because even if she doesn't do well as a racehorse or even make it to the racetrack, she still has a chance to be a good producer, provided she has a decent pedigree and conformation. The ideal broodmare prospect, of course, is one with an impressive race record and plenty of quality in her pedigree.

If you are just entering the breeding business, broodmare prospects, especially lesser-performing fillies bought off the track, can be more economical. However, you have no breeding history to go on and the mare could have fertility problems. Before purchasing a filly or mare privately, you can have a veterinarian check for breeding soundness; however, breeding soundness does not guarantee that the mare won't have fertility problems. If you decide to claim a filly or mare from a race, be aware that the horse comes "as is" and is yours as soon as the starting gate opens. *(See Chapter 2 for more about claiming.)*

2) Barren mares: Mares that have been bred but for whatever reason did not get or stay in foal are called "barren" for that breed-

THINGS TO KNOW

Buying a Mare

- Determine your goal — breed to sell, breed to race, etc.
- Set a budget.
- Find a reputable adviser. (Your state owner/breeder association is a good resource. See Resources for more information.)
- Do your homework before making a purchase!

ing season. Sometimes a mare just naturally takes a break and won't get pregnant, but in other cases, a serious health problem could be the cause. Examine a mare's produce record (listed on her sales catalog page or obtained from a statistical resource such as EquineLine or Bloodstock Research). Does she have a number of "barren" or "foal aborted" years? These could indicate she is a "problem" mare, with fertility or other health issues.

3) Mares in foal: If you buy a mare in foal, you will hopefully get a little bonus a few months later in a healthy colt or filly. (As the new mare owner, you will be the official breeder of that foal you bought *in utero*.) If buying privately, you should have a veterinarian confirm the mare's status before buying her. In sales catalogs, mares are listed as "believed to be pregnant" (along with the name of the stallion to whom they have been bred). Prior to the sale, familiarize yourself with the sales company's conditions of sale, especially its policies on broodmares and on veterinary examinations for determining in-foal status. In-foal mares come in all price ranges depending on their pedigree, conformation, previous offsprings' racing ability, and so on.

Criteria for Choosing a Mare

When looking at the type of mares you'd like to purchase, you should also consider various criteria before making your decision. Some key elements include price level, pedigree, conformation, racing and/or breeding performance, and breeding health.

Price: How much money are you willing to spend? Or how much can you afford to spend? Be realistic about price level and what kind of mares you can get for your money. Say you have a budget of $20,000. You could either buy one decent mare for that amount or

ANNE M. EBERHARDT

Buying an in-foal mare can result in a bonus foal come spring several cheaper mares (and this is where a reputable adviser can help with these decisions), but regardless, you have to shop in the appropriate places and find the best mare in your price range.

Pedigree: Most mating planners and pedigree consultants tell you that if a mare doesn't have some black type in her first two dams on a catalog page, then look elsewhere. (Black type has become synonymous with stakes winners because in a sales catalog, stakes winners' names are listed in all upper case, boldface type. Stakes-placed horses are listed in upper/lower case, boldface type.

BENOIT & ASSOCIATES

You can buy mares off the racetrack

The International Cataloguing Standards Committee of the Society of International Thoroughbred Auctioneers determines which stakes races around the world qualify for black type.) Sometimes the cheaper a mare is, the harder it is to find that important black type close up in the pedigree; however, if a cheap mare all you can afford, then look for the pedigree's good points: Is the sire line known for getting sound runners? Are there any current producing daughters in the female family? What kind of runners does the family produce? Would a foal from this family be salable (if that is your goal)?

Conformation: Good conformation is important, no matter what sex/age horse you're trying to buy. As with humans, some horses have an athletic physique and the talent to go with it, while others, through hard work and patient training, are able to overcome physical deficiencies and achieve success. But some physical deficiencies or conformation faults, such as having severely offset knees or being back at the knee, are more serious than others and can lead to unsoundness or injury, and thus are not desirable traits to pass on.

If you are not familiar with evaluating horses' conformation, find a reliable adviser to guide you. However, you can develop your own eye for a good horse by studying drawings of ideal conformation and the main faults *(See Chapter 5 for more on conformation.)* and then going to a sale and looking at lots of horses to see how they stack up. Broodmares who had racetrack success probably have fairly good conformation, but many broodmares didn't make it to the track or only raced once or twice before being injured and poor conformation might be the reason.

Racing performance: The late Joe Estes, a longtime editor of *The Blood-Horse* who wrote extensively on pedigrees and breeding, was a proponent of buying successful race mares as potential broodmares, and a good race record, including black type, is certainly something you should look for. A solid race record indicates a talent and affinity for racing — something not all Thoroughbreds have — as well as an ability to withstand the rigors of the racetrack. The hope is that those traits will be passed to any offspring. However, finding a mare with a solid race career may not be feasible so this is where pedigree can come in. Does the mare have any siblings or half siblings that have won or that are winning on the track? Are there any stakes performers? How many starts have they made (an indicator of soundness)? Did the mare or her siblings win at two and three or as older horses, i.e., precocity versus late-development?

Breeding performance: Instead of a maiden (unbred) mare, you might want to purchase an older mare that has a proven produce record. Mares between ages 12 and 15 should have already produced several foals of racing age. Even better is the mare whose offspring actually raced and won. With a proven broodmare, you know she can produce winners and hopefully will continue to do so. A caveat to this is that an increase in age is associated with a decrease in fertility, so the older the mare, the less likely she'll continue to produce at the level she did when she was younger. This is not always the case, of course, because there are no absolutes in breeding

ANNE M. EBERHARDT

You can find mares in all price ranges at public auction

horses. Somethingroyal was 18 when she foaled Secretariat, but don't pin your hopes on buying an older mare just to get the next Big Red.

Breeding health: Be sure to consider the mare's overall health and fertility. An older mare's produce record may indicate fertility issues if she has several barren years. If

Consigned by Katalpa Farm (Lonnie R. Owens), Agent VII

Barn 28 | **Hip No. 997**

HOLY MIA

Gray or Roan Mare; foaled 1997

HOLY MIA	Holy Bull	Great Above	Minnesota Mac
			Ta Wee
		Sharon Brown	Al Hattab
			Agathea's Dawn
	Mia Karina (1983)	Icecapade	Nearctic
			Shenanigans
		Basin	Tom Rolfe
			Delta

By HOLY BULL (1991). Horse of the year, stakes winner of $2,481,760, Travers S. **[G1]**, etc. Sire of 8 crops of racing age, 525 foals, 363 starters, 23 stakes winners, 244 winners of 697 races and earning $22,036,220 & $154,110(CAN) in N.A., including champion Macho Uno ($1,851,803, Breeders' Cup Juvenile **[G1]**, etc.), and of Dream Chief **[G2]** (hwt. in Italy), Giacomo **[G1]** ($1,966,316), Confessional **[G1]**. Sire of dams of stakes winners Higher World, Tani Maru, General Charley, Chocolate Brown.

1st dam

MIA KARINA, by Icecapade. Winner at 3 in France. Dam of 6 other registered foals, 6 of racing age, 5 to race, 5 winners, including--

SIBERIAN SUMMER (c. by Siberian Express). 6 wins, 3 to 6, $501,615, Charles H. Strub S. **[G1]**, 2nd Bay Meadows Derby **[G3]**, Volante H. **[G3]**, El Cajon S.-R (DMR, $11,000). Sire.

MAGNIFICIENT STYLE (f. by Silver Hawk). 2 wins in 4 starts at 3 in England, Tattersalls Musidora S. **[G3]**, 3rd R. L. Davison Pretty Polly S.; placed at 4, $27,290, in N.A. Dam of 5 foals, 4 winners--

PLAYFUL ACT (f. by Sadler's Wells). 4 wins in 6 starts at 2 and 3, 2005 in England, hwt. filly at 2 on English Hand., Meon Valley Stud Mile **[G1]**, etc.; placed at 3, 2005 in Ireland, 2nd Darley Irish Oaks **[G1]**.

PERCUSSIONIST (g. by Sadler's Wells). 2 wins at 3, placed at 4, 2005 in England, Gallagher Group Ltd. Derby Trial S. **[G3]**, etc.; placed at 3 in France, 3rd Prix Chaudenay Casino Barriere de Menton **[G2]**.

ECHOES IN ETERNITY (f. by Spinning World). 4 wins, 2 to 4 in England, National Stud Never Say Die Club Park Hill S. **[G2]**, etc.

STYLELISTICK (f. by Storm Cat). 4 wins at 2 and 3, $234,788, Green River S. [L] (KEE, $70,618), Appalachian S. [L] (KEE, $69,502), 3rd Regret S. **[G3]** (CD, $16,905).

Kelly Or Rae (c. by Green Forest). 13 wins, 2 to 10, $122,524.

2nd dam

BASIN, by Tom Rolfe. Half-sister to **DIKE** ($351,274), **CANAL**, **CABILDO**, **OKAVANGO**, **SHORE**, **Moss**. Dam of 9 foals to race, 8 winners, incl.--

Copperhead. 2 wins. Dam of **SILVER ENDING [G1]** (c. by Silver Hawk).

RACE RECORD: At 2, one win. Earned $28,236.

PRODUCE RECORD:

2001 Speedy Sunrise, f. by Cherokee Run. Winner at 3 and 4, 2005, $64,717.

2002 Hey Doll, f. by Siphon (BRZ). Winner at 3, 2005, $13,414.

2003 Gonfer, c. by Mt. Livermore. Winner at 2, 2005 in Mexico.

2004 f. by Orientate; 2005 c. by Stormin Fever.

Mated to Medaglia d'Oro (El Prado (IRE)--Cappucino Bay), last service May 18, 2005. (Believed to be **PREGNANT**).

NTRA.

Review a mare's produce record on her sales catalog page

you plan to buy a mare privately, you should consider arranging a purchase examination and/or breeding soundness examination by your vet. These examinations are designed to help you make a more informed buying decision.

A breeding soundness exam is probably needed more for an older mare or one with a breeding history indicating fertility problems; young, maiden mares usually don't need this exam if they are otherwise healthy, but it is always a good practice to consult your veterinarian before any horse purchase. Among the procedures a vet will perform during a breeding soundness exam are recording a mare's breeding and foaling history, pal-

Business and Tax Considerations

Well in advance of buying your first broodmare, you need to make some key business decisions.

Foremost, you must determine whether you want to breed as a hobby or as a business. Most people choose to breed horses as a business because of tax and liability considerations.

You can choose among several ways to establish a business. Though you can operate as a sole proprietor, doing business as a corporation or partnership probably makes better business sense.

Options include the following:

- sole proprietorship
- C corporation — limits the liability of shareholders; corporation pays taxes, meaning shareholders do not get to deduct corporation's losses on their own tax returns.
- S corporation — similar to a partnership in that the corporation's income and losses can be passed on to individual shareholders.
- general partnership — at least two individuals join together; partnership files its own tax returns; all income and losses are passed on to the partners.
- limited partnership — requires a general partner; limited partners do not participate in management; limits partners' liability to their investment.
- limited liability company — like a partnership, income and losses passed through to the partners.
- limited liability partnerships — similar to a general partnership but individual partners are not liable for the actions of other partners.

Each entity has its requirements and tax treatments. Consult with a tax adviser before choosing an option that works best for you. *(See Resources for recommended reading on entering the Thoroughbred business.)*

THINGS TO KNOW

The American Horse Council publishes two books on equine tax issues: *Horse Owners and Breeders Tax Handbook* and a condensed version, *Tax Tips for Horse Owners*. Contact the horse council at (202) 296-4031.

Hobby Loss/Passive Loss

The Internal Revenue Service carefully scrutinizes new small businesses to ensure compliance with federal hobby loss rules. The burden is on the taxpayer to show that he or she is really operating a business rather than indulging in a hobby. The taxpayer must demonstrate his intention

pating the reproductive tract, examining the vulvar conformation; taking a uterine swab for bacteria culture, etc. *(See Chapter 9.)*

The American Association of Equine Practitioners recommends the following guidelines for a thorough purchase and/or breeding soundness exam:

- Explain to your vet your goals for the horse (e.g., racing, breeding).
- Have your vet outline which procedures he or she will include in the exam and why.
- Establish the costs for the exam.
- Be present during the exam. The seller or agent should also be present.
- Discuss the vet's findings in private.

Mares consigned to a public

of making a profit. This means the taxpayer must show a profit in at least two out of any seven consecutive years beginning with the first loss year.

The taxpayer also must show his involvement in his horse business to deduct losses against earned income. Passive loss rules require owners to show "material participation" in the business. This generally means 500 hours a year.

THINGS TO KNOW

Hobby or Business?

The IRS cites nine factors in determining whether an activity is a hobby or business. They include the following:

- time and effort spent in the activity
- the taxpayer's degree of knowledge
- expectation of making a profit
- the taxpayer's history of income or losses

Depreciation

Horses generally can be depreciated over three to seven years. Racehorses older than two and breeding horses older than 12 are depreciated over three years. Here is a depreciation schedule for a broodmare under age 12:

Year	*% of original cost to be depreciated*
1	10.715%
2	19.134%
3	15.033%
4	12.248%
5	12.248%
6	12.248%
7	12.248%
8	6.128%

Capital Gains

The current capital gains rate is 15 percent. Under the current tax code, the holding period for long-term capital gains treatment on horses is 24 months instead of the 12 months for other assets used in trade or business. Efforts have been under way in Congress to make capital gains treatment of horses the more favorable 12 months. This reduced holding period would result in much more favorable federal tax savings for individuals in higher income brackets.

By Jacqueline Duke

auction are sold under the sales company's conditions of sale, which govern all aspects of the sale process including which veterinary procedures/surgeries must be announced, and in the case of broodmares, certification that a mare is pregnant and a purchaser's recourse if the mare is found after purchase not to be pregnant. Definitions for "pregnant," "not pregnant," "aborted," "suitable for mating," and so on adhere to guidelines established by the AAEP. *(See Chapter 2 for an example from Keeneland's conditions of sale.)*

As you delve into the world of Thoroughbred breeding, you will determine which criteria are most important to you and your goals and how to weight those criteria when evaluating mares. Next comes the decision of where to buy — privately, public auction, or perhaps through a claiming race.

By Judy L. Marchman

Buying a Mare

You can purchase a Thoroughbred mare in three venues: 1) at a public auction, 2) by private sale, and 3) in a claiming race. Auctions are the most convenient venue because they bring a large number of mares together in one place. Buyers can compare conformation and temperament as well as pedigree and produce records, the latter two being provided on the catalog page. Buying at auction also is the safest approach for a newcomer to purchase a broodmare prospect; claiming is the riskiest way.

Public Auctions

Major Sales vs. Regional Sales

Thoroughbred auctions that sell broodmares and broodmare prospects are conducted throughout the fall and winter, beginning in October and running through February. These sales are variously called breeding stock and mixed sales. The major auction companies are Keeneland and Fasig-Tipton Company, both of which have their offices in Kentucky.

In addition to the major auctions, regional auctions are conducted by state breeder associations, such as the Minnesota Thoroughbred Association and the Washington Thoroughbred Breeders Association, and by regional sales companies, such as Barretts Equine Limited, in California, and the Ocala Breeders' Sales Company, in Florida. The latter two hold mixed sales in January and again in October. Fasig-Tipton, in addition to a major sale in November, conducts a winter mixed sale in Kentucky in February, and regional mixed sales in Maryland and Texas every December, and again in Maryland in February.

Catalog offerings vary in size and quality, depending upon the sale, and even upon the specific session of a particular sale. Catalog quality refers to pedigree and other characteristics of the mares selling in a particular session, such as race record, produce record, and physical appearance. Major sales catalogs offer top quality and are well stocked, making those sales a good place to hunt for value.

For example, the Keeneland November breeding stock and January horses of all ages sales are the two largest venues for broodmares and broodmare prospects in the country, with thousands of mares offered at each. The 2006 January sale spanned seven days during which 1,624 head sold from 2,508 head cataloged for an average price of $44,443 and a median price of $16,000. The 2005 November sale required 12 days, and resulted in 2,816 head sold from 4,477 head cataloged, for an average price of $102,842 and a median price of $35,000.

Catalog quality is higher in the earlier days of the Keeneland sales and prices tend to be higher on those days. Study the summary

ANNE M. EBERHARDT

Mares sold at auctions have to be certified by vets as pregnant or not pregnant

sheets for these bigger sales and you will see that each session's average and median prices drop as the sale progresses. Day one of the 2005 November sale resulted in a $545,117 average and $315,000 median price, while day 12 saw an $8,078 average and a $4,200 median.

Fasig-Tipton's November mixed sale is a single-day sale of several hundred head that results in a six-digit average price. This sale precedes Keeneland's November sale.

Regional sales, by comparison, serve the breeding and racing industry in a specific area. Prices tend to be more down to earth and more in line with the closing days of the Keeneland November sale. Regional sale prices can range from five digits to three.

Because pedigrees in regional markets can vary substantially in value, it pays to know the leading sires and female families in a particular region. *The Blood-Horse* periodically publishes lists of leading sires in regional markets; regional leading sires lists also are available at www.bloodhorse.com.

Catalog size for regional sales can range from less than 100 to a few hundred head.

Conditions of Sale

When you buy at public auction, risk is reduced because a sales company requires a veterinary certificate from consignors that any mare being sold as pregnant is indeed pregnant and any mare being sold as not pregnant is suitable for mating. Here, it is time for you as a buyer to turn to the conditions of sale set forth by all sales companies. Conditions of sale address credit and payment, responsibilities of the buyer and seller, warranties concerning soundness, and steps for resolving disputes.

The sales companies are similar in regard to protecting buyers, but you should read each company's conditions of sale thoroughly before you steam ahead to the bidding, as there might be some differences in the language. Conditions of sale are printed toward the front of the sales catalogs; Keeneland's sales conditions are also posted on Keeneland's Web site at www.keeneland.com.

Keeneland, which annually sells more than $300-million worth of breeding stock in addition to yearlings and two-year-olds in training, covers special provisions for broodmares under its Twelfth Condition of Sale. This states that to be certified as pregnant, a mare must be found to be pregnant in the opinion of the examining veterinarian, based on manual examination performed within 10 days prior to the sale date. For a mare to be certified as suitable for mating, a rectal palpation and speculum examination performed within 10 days prior to the sale date must not reveal any significant abnormalities of the reproductive system. Furthermore, a buyer may have any mare examined by a veterinarian before she is removed from the sale premises and within 24 hours after the end of the session in which she was sold. If the broodmare is found to be not as certified, she may, at the option of the buyer, be returned to the consignor.

Fasig-Tipton has its protective language under its sixth condition of sale — limited warranties as to broodmares. Barretts Equine Limited extends this protection to buyers under its eleventh condition of sale. Both Fasig-Tipton and Barretts allow for a return within 10 days of the sale if the mare is found to be not as certified when examined within 24 hours of purchase and before leaving the sales grounds.

Even with the veterinary certificate the auction company requires, it is a good practice to have a reproductive veterinarian do a

TWELFTH

SPECIAL PROVISIONS FOR BROODMARES: Each broodmare i... sale shall be offered with veterinary certificate provided by the consignor in conformity with standards established by the American Association of Equine Practitioners, showing her to be either (1) pregnant, in the opinion of the examining veterinarian, based on manual examination within ten (10) days prior to the date of sale, or (2) not pregnant, but suitable for mating in the opinion of the examining veterinarian based upon appropriate examination with ten (10) days prior to the date of sale. It is further agreed that the purchaser may have any broodmare examined by a veterinarian before the broodmare is removed from the sale premises and within twenty-four (24) hours after the end of the session in which the broodmare was sold. If the purchaser's veterinarian finds the broodmare not to be as certified and if the consignor's veterinarian continues to disagree, then Keeneland will appoint a third veterinarian whose certificate in these circumstances, shall be **final, binding and conclusive** upon consignor, purchaser and all other parties absent fraud or bad faith. If the broodmare is found to be not as certified, pursuant to the above procedures, she may, at the option of purchaser, be returned to the consignor as unsold. If she is found to be pregnant, when sold as not pregnant, the purchaser may, as stated above, rescind the sale or may accept the sale, but in that event the purchaser shall pay the applicable stud fee, plus Kentucky sales tax. If she is found to be as certified ... haser shall be require... lete the purch... the

The Twelfth Condition of Sale from a Keeneland sales catalog

1 The number identifying the horse, appearing on its hip.

2 The horse's pedigree, traced three generations. At each generation the sire appears on the top and the dam on the bottom.

3 A synopsis of the sire's racing record and notable progeny.

4 A synopsis of the first dam's racing record and progeny.

5 The subject mare's race record.

6 The subject mare's produce record, shown by year foaled.

7 The produce record also shows years in which the subject mare did not deliver a foal and gives the reason as reported by the mare owner to The Jockey Club.

8 The name of the stallion to whom the subject mare has been bred and the date of the last mating.

9 Indicates whether the subject mare, based on recent veterinary examination, is thought to be in foal to the stallion listed as "mated to."

10 Bold capital letters for a horse's name indicate the horse is a stakes winner. If its name appears in bold lower-case letters, the horse is stakes-placed.

11 The horse's birth date, or in this case, the year foaled.

12 The horse's name. If unnamed, the horse is described by sex and color.

13 The name of the consignor (the farm or individual selling the horse).

14 The barn number where the consignor is located.

BROODMARE
Catalog Page

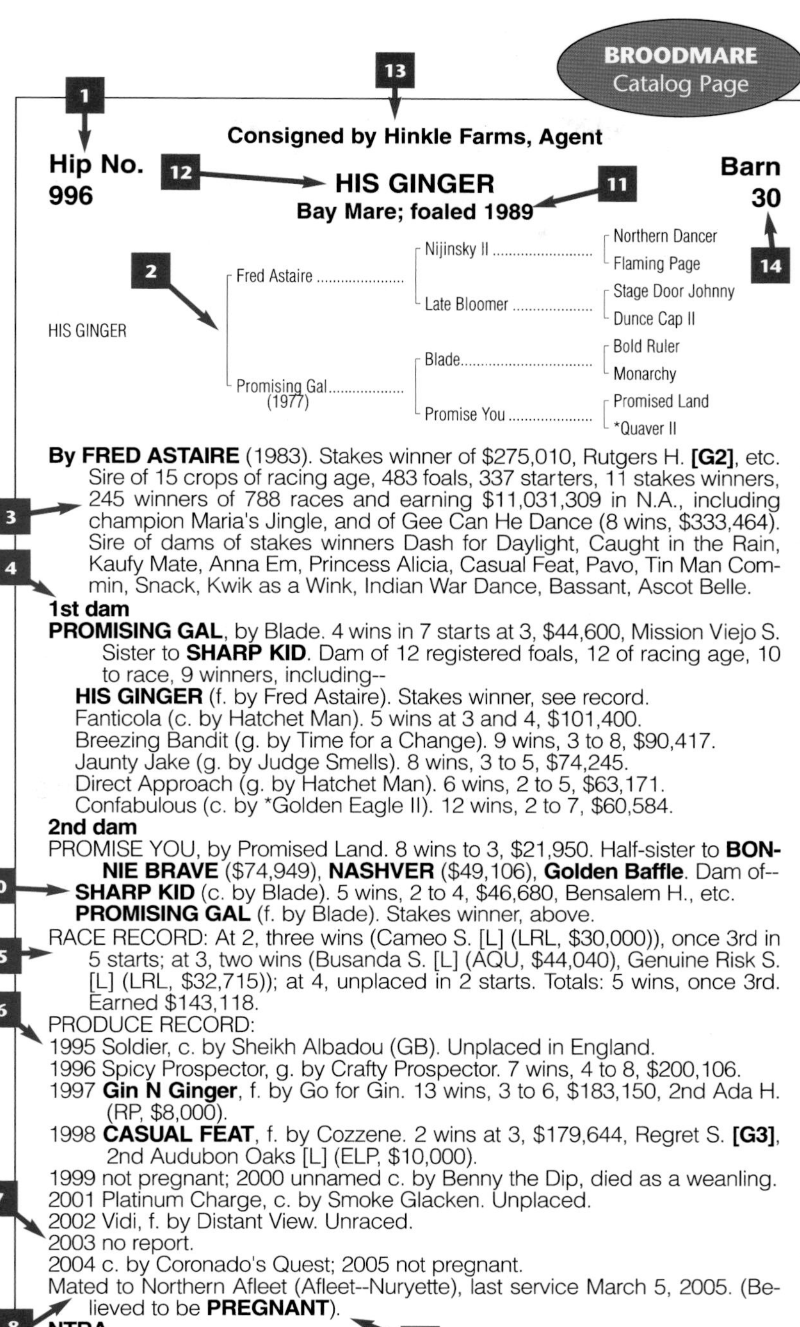

Consigned by Hinkle Farms, Agent

Hip No. 996

Barn 30

HIS GINGER
Bay Mare; foaled 1989

HIS GINGER
- Fred Astaire
  - Nijinsky II
    - Northern Dancer
    - Flaming Page
  - Late Bloomer
    - Stage Door Johnny
    - Dunce Cap II
- Promising Gal (1977)
  - Blade
    - Bold Ruler
    - Monarchy
  - Promise You
    - Promised Land
    - *Quaver II

By FRED ASTAIRE (1983). Stakes winner of $275,010, Rutgers H. **[G2]**, etc. Sire of 15 crops of racing age, 483 foals, 337 starters, 11 stakes winners, 245 winners of 788 races and earning $11,031,309 in N.A., including champion Maria's Jingle, and of Gee Can He Dance (8 wins, $333,464). Sire of dams of stakes winners Dash for Daylight, Caught in the Rain, Kaufy Mate, Anna Em, Princess Alicia, Casual Feat, Pavo, Tin Man Commin, Snack, Kwik as a Wink, Indian War Dance, Bassant, Ascot Belle.

1st dam

PROMISING GAL, by Blade. 4 wins in 7 starts at 3, $44,600, Mission Viejo S. Sister to **SHARP KID**. Dam of 12 registered foals, 12 of racing age, 10 to race, 9 winners, including--

HIS GINGER (f. by Fred Astaire). Stakes winner, see record.
Fanticola (c. by Hatchet Man). 5 wins at 3 and 4, $101,400.
Breezing Bandit (g. by Time for a Change). 9 wins, 3 to 8, $90,417.
Jaunty Jake (g. by Judge Smells). 8 wins, 3 to 5, $74,245.
Direct Approach (g. by Hatchet Man). 6 wins, 2 to 5, $63,171.
Confabulous (c. by *Golden Eagle II). 12 wins, 2 to 7, $60,584.

2nd dam

PROMISE YOU, by Promised Land. 8 wins to 3, $21,950. Half-sister to **BONNIE BRAVE** ($74,949), **NASHVER** ($49,106), **Golden Baffle**. Dam of--
SHARP KID (c. by Blade). 5 wins, 2 to 4, $46,680, Bensalem H., etc.
PROMISING GAL (f. by Blade). Stakes winner, above.

RACE RECORD: At 2, three wins (Cameo S. [L] (LRL, $30,000)), once 3rd in 5 starts; at 3, two wins (Busanda S. [L] (AQU, $44,040), Genuine Risk S. [L] (LRL, $32,715)); at 4, unplaced in 2 starts. Totals: 5 wins, once 3rd. Earned $143,118.

PRODUCE RECORD:
1995 Soldier, c. by Sheikh Albadou (GB). Unplaced in England.
1996 Spicy Prospector, g. by Crafty Prospector. 7 wins, 4 to 8, $200,106.
1997 **Gin N Ginger**, f. by Go for Gin. 13 wins, 3 to 6, $183,150, 2nd Ada H. (RP, $8,000).
1998 **CASUAL FEAT**, f. by Cozzene. 2 wins at 3, $179,644, Regret S. **[G3]**, 2nd Audubon Oaks [L] (ELP, $10,000).
1999 not pregnant; 2000 unnamed c. by Benny the Dip, died as a weanling.
2001 Platinum Charge, c. by Smoke Glacken. Unplaced.
2002 Vidi, f. by Distant View. Unraced.
2003 no report.
2004 c. by Coronado's Quest; 2005 not pregnant.
Mated to Northern Afleet (Afleet--Nuryette), last service March 5, 2005. (Believed to be **PREGNANT**).

NTRA.

($358,951, champion twice in Canada), **MISS**
keg, **Victorian Host**. Dam of 11 foals, 8 to race, all win...
VICTORIAN QUEEN. 12 wins to 4, $188,019, champion gras...
champion handicap mare in Canada, Ontario Sire S.-R, etc. Dam
JUDGE ANGELUCCI [G1] ($1,582,535), **WAR [G1]** ($377,832), **PEACE [G1]** ($361,950). Granddam of **EXHAUST NOTE**, **GRADUATED**, etc.
DUNDRUM DANCER. Stakes winner, above.
Lady Sylvie. 3 wins to 3, $21,508. Dam of **Devil's Fire** [L] ($267,362), **Slewpy Slew** ($192,327), **Sweet Native Lady** ($19,060, dam of **Sweet Defense** [L], $111,614). Granddam of **Sajana** (hwt. at 3 on Italian Hand., 14 fur. & up), **ROY'S TRIGGER** ($112,755), **Fit to Be a Gent** ($182,285).
Queen Magi. Unraced. Granddam of **COURTLY NATIVE** (dam of **COURTLY KATHY**, $277,950; **Talaris [G3]**, $103,355; **Mystic Diablo**, $93,324).
RACE RECORD: At 2, unraced; at 3, three wins, twice 2nd (Black-Eyed Susan S. **[G2]** (PIM, $40,000), Federico Tesio S. [L] (PIM, $20,000)), once 3rd (Wide Country S. (LRL, $4,400)); at 4, 2005, one win in 2 starts. Totals: 4 wins, twice 2nd, once 3rd. Earned $137,630.
Mated to Grand Slam (Gone West--Bright Candles), last service April 16, 2005. (Believed to be not pregnant).

Example of a cataloged mare noted as "not pregnant"

thorough examination of any mare you purchase at auction prior to her removal from the sales grounds. Better still, the physical should be part of a pre-purchase exam in which her overall health is evaluated.

Perusing the Catalog

The astute horseman can find a bargain at every auction. Good horses sometimes just get overlooked. But while bargains can be found, auctions are often charged with their own dynamics and drama that electrify the bidding and drive up the prices on particular mares. The best plan for buying wisely at auction is to select ahead of time a few mares that you believe will be in your price range. You and/or your adviser should go and look at the mares on your list and compare them.

A broodmare catalog page *(see previous page)* will give the subject mare's hip number, year of birth, a three-generation pedigree, and her race and produce records. It will give a synopsis of the racing and progeny records of the subject mare's sire and dam. If the mare is pregnant, the covering sire, plus the date of her last service, is given on the bottom line. If the mare is open (not in foal), the bottom line will give the reason.

When you like what you see on the catalog page in terms of pedigree, produce record, the mare's age, the stallion to whom the mare is in foal, etc., you can add the mare to the list of hip numbers you want to inspect. The top of the catalog page will tell you the name of the consignor selling the horse and the number of the barn where you can find her. (Sales catalogs often have maps of the barns.)

Inspecting Mares

In a public auction, horses are required to be on the grounds at least a day prior to selling so that buyers can inspect them. When you arrive at the sale barn, you will probably will be given a pre-printed card listing the horses in that consignment. You should check off the hip numbers of the horses you want to see and sign the card in the space provided.

For any horse you are considering, the pre-purchase inspection begins with an evaluation of its conformation or physical makeup. A conformation evaluation involves studying the horse while it is standing still on level ground; looking at it from the front, rear, and side; and then watching it walk away and back toward you. Conformation is the relationship of form to function, which is the reason that seeing the horse move is useful for evaluation. *(See Chapter 5 for discussion of conformation.)*

In addition to looking at a mare's overall physical conformation, breeders look under the tail and inspect the reproductive conformation of any mare they are considering for broodmare purposes. This is different from the veterinary examination we discussed earlier that includes palpating the ovaries, which of course should be part of the inspection process. Reproductive conformation refers specifically to whether the mare's vulva is vertical or tipped back. If the vulva is tipped back, the mare will be vulnerable to reproductive tract infections due to feces being sucked in after she defecates. Infections make it difficult or impossible to get a mare in foal or carry a foal to term. Often, a tipped-back vulva can be managed with a Caslick's stitch, a procedure in which the vulvar lips are surgically cut, and the top two-thirds are sewn together so that the vulva will seal together as it heals. (Enough space is left open for urine and discharge to pass. The stitch must be opened by a veterinarian prior to foaling.) But even with a Caslick's stitch these mares are considered to be high risk. Whether buying at auction or in a private sale, breeders will check a mare's reproductive conformation.

Mixed sales bring another dimension to the inspection process. Often, a mare and her

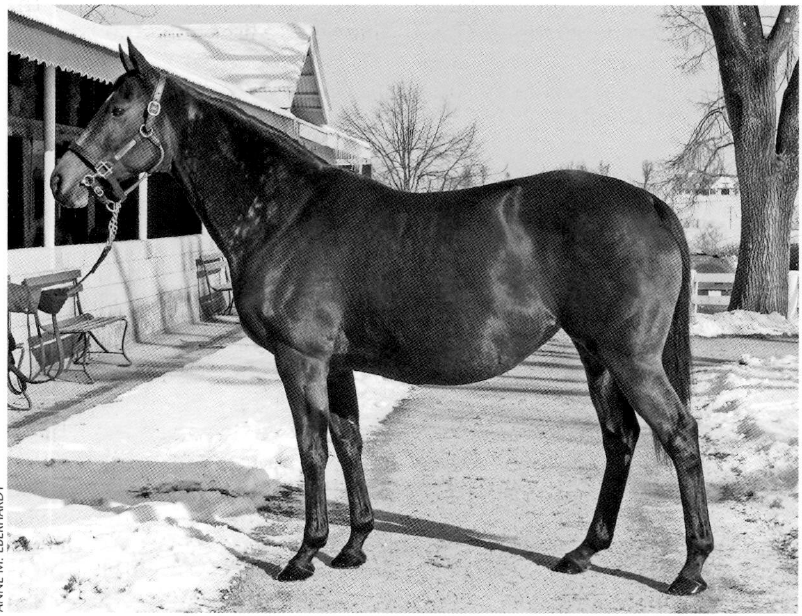

ANNE M. EBERHARDT

You can inspect a mare before she goes through the sales ring

weanling will sell in the same session (usually by the same consignor), so you can get a look at a foal out of a mare you are considering. This gives you an opportunity to see what physical and temperamental characteristics the mare might pass on to any foal she produces for you.

At this point, having inspected and compared a few mares, you are ready to put a figure on what you will be comfortable paying for each mare.

Private Sale

One place to find mares for sale privately is in the classified ads in the back of *The Blood-Horse* or other Thoroughbred trade magazines, and in local newspapers. But you are not restricted to mares that are advertised for sale. You may make a reasonable offer on any mare. You can contact breeding farms directly to let them know you are in the market for a mare and what your budget is. Bloodstock agents are another source for buying privately. Some will have horses for sale, and others can play a vital role in finding and inspecting prospects for you.

If you are interested in purchasing a particular mare, contact the owner, trainer, or owner's agent; if the mare has not been advertised, inquire if she is for sale. If she is, the next step is to inspect the mare. Evaluate her conformation. When you are buying privately, as part of a pre-purchase exam it is especially important to hire a vet to examine the mare to evaluate her reproductive ability and her overall health. Next, decide if you are comfortable with the asking price or determine an amount that reflects the quality of the mare's pedigree, conformation, race record, and produce record — if she has any foals of racing age. Once you have an offering price, you (or your agent) are ready to make a formal offer. For this, the Thoroughbred Owners and Breeders Association's Web site (www.toba.org) provides the following information:

"A written Agreement of Sale or Purchase should be prepared and should include the names of the parties, identification of the horse, terms of sale, warranties of sale, contingencies and deadlines and site of the transaction, as sales tax may be a factor. It may be prudent to also include a procedure for resolving disputes, as well as a provision acknowledging the right for a complete veterinary examination. In most cases insurance providers require a veterinary examination before a policy will be issued. Where questions or suspicions exist, good business practice suggests that a title search should be made to ascertain that the seller's title is free of liens.

"Upon acceptance of the offer, the purchaser should request a Bill of Sale. A Security Agreement may be imposed by the seller to secure payment if the seller finances any portion of the purchase price. At the closing, the purchaser should receive the horse's Jockey Club Certificate, as well as copies of its health records."

Another place where mares sometimes sell privately might surprise newcomers to the industry — auctions. It is not always the case that all horses on the sales grounds change owners in the auction ring. Private sales take place there, too. Here's how it works.

A mare can be led out of the sale ring unsold if the bidding does not meet the minimum price or reserve that her consignor filed with the sales office before she went to the ring. The bid board will display what appears to be a final bid. To find out if a mare actually did sell, you would consult the sales office, or the sale summary sheet, which the sales office makes available at the end of each session. "RNA," short for "reserve not attained," appears on the summary sheet at some sales companies. "Not Sold" appears on others. Once you or your agent has determined that a mare was not sold, it is often just a matter of walking back to the sale barn and finding the consignor to negotiate a price and complete the transaction.

Claiming

Claiming races make up the majority of races run in the United States every year. (There are actually three types of claiming races. Besides the standard kind, maiden claiming races are specifically for horses that have never won, and optional claiming races, the least common variety, are a hybrid race, in which horses that are not for sale also may be entered.)

Claiming races typically bring together horses that have inconsistent racing form, and as a result are not quite good enough to compete in allowance or stakes races. From this simple truth the phrase "dropped into a claiming race" evolved.

In a claiming race, the horses that are entered are for sale to eligible buyers for a specified price that is stated in the program. When you claim a horse, you buy it.

The rules of racing dictate who is eligible to put in a claim. These rules vary from track to track, but if you are new to the industry, you will need to enlist a licensed horseman — either a trainer or owner who meets the requirements for claiming at that track — to make the claim for you.

THINGS TO KNOW

Claiming Races

- Claiming races can be a good source for future broodmares.
- Claiming prices range from $1,500 to $100,000 or more.
- Risks include the possibility that the filly could have reproductive issues and that she could be injured in the race from which she is claimed.
- Before claiming a filly, review pertinent pedigree information.

Claiming prices vary from track to track and range from $5,000 to $150,000. The Jockey Club Information Services reported there were 13,870 claiming races restricted just to fillies and mares in the U.S. in 2005. There were 14,404 in 2004; 14,246 in 2003; and 14,275 in 2002.

The opportunity to obtain a good broodmare prospect from a claiming race is there, and possibly at a discount. Look at these examples:

Bonnie's Poker won 11 of 63 starts and earned more than $150,000 in the mid-1980s. She raced for a "tag" — that is, in a claiming race — in every one of her last 33 starts, for prices ranging from $22,500 down to $12,000. But her real claim to fame is as a broodmare. Bonnie's Poker is the dam of Silver Charm, winner of the 1997 Kentucky Derby and Preakness and 1998 Dubai World Cup. Prior to Silver Charm's success, other foals out of Bonnie's Poker didn't inspire much enthusiasm at public auction. Caught

A claim box

Bluffing sold as a two-year-old at the 1994 Ocala Breeders' Sales Co.'s April sale for a mere $1,600. Even Silver Charm himself brought only $16,500 as a yearling, though he did bring $100,000 as an impressive two-year-old. But at the 1997 Keeneland September yearling sale, Bonnie's Poker's filly, Silver Chance, brought $125,000 and in 2000 her yearling filly, Elrose, sold for $700,000.

Thorough Fair, now the dam of two graded stakes winners in WhyWhyWhy and Spellbinder, was claimed out of a race by James E. Jones for a mere $5,000 in 1997. Jones, a farrier, acquired her as a broodmare prospect. After selling three of her first five foals at Keeneland for a cumulative $1,065,000 (the first one to sell, Spellbinder, sold during WhyWhyWhy's graded stakes winning two-year-old season in 2002), Jones sold Thorough Fair, in foal to Giant's Causeway, at the 2005 Keeneland November sale, for $825,000.

Often, fillies from good families — fillies that might have sold for pretty pennies as babies — wind up getting dropped into claiming races when allowance races prove too tough, and their owners are willing to drop them in class in order to pick up a check.

Although you won't find the kind of detailed pedigree information you need in the *Daily Racing Form,* the periodical does give the auction price if the filly sold as a weanling, yearling, or two-year-old in training. The more somebody paid for her before she raced, the more likely she was considered a good individual conformation-wise and/or has a half or full sibling in her pedigree that will be meaningful to buyers when her offspring go to sell. But you will want to check up on this.

Remember that entries come out two or three days prior to the race, and that leeway gives you time to do your pedigree homework. Pedigree information is available through several sources *(See Resources for more information)*. The Jockey Club's EquineLine is one source where you can obtain a variety of reports such as the dam's produce record, and you can even request a catalog page for the filly you are interested in. The cost per report will vary, depending upon the product chosen. American Produce Records, available on CD-ROM, provides race and produce records on 1.2 million Thoroughbreds and is updated annually. Several annual supplements published by Blood-Horse Publications, specifically *Nicks, Sires, Dams, Auctions,* and the *Stallion Register,* provide pedigree information.

But before you put in a claim, beware. There is risk.

When you claim a filly or mare out of a race, there is always a chance that she might have fertility problems. (Paradoxically, normal heat cycles can keep a filly or mare from performing well, so the reason she has a poor race record might mean that she will at least be fertile.) She could have undeveloped, infantile ovaries — "the size of a pea," to cite breeders and reproductive vets — and you would have no recourse as far as returning her.

Very athletic fillies in hard training sometimes stop cycling naturally. After being at the track they might simply need time before they ovulate normally. In other cases, the reproductive system goes dormant due to the practice some racing stables have of administering anabolic steroids to fillies to increase weight and suppress the estrous (heat) cycle. Equipoise and Winstrol V are two anabolic steroid products often used in this fashion. A filly started on anabolic steroids young and kept on them for a long time might need a season for her estrous cycle to get back on track. This is a risk you take when you claim, especially if you are planning to get her in foal right away.

You could ask the trainer if you can have a vet perform a pre-purchase exam that involves palpating the mare's ovaries. Keep in mind, however, that you are then telling the trainer that someone is serious about claiming a filly or mare that, despite running for a price, the stable might actually want to keep.

Claiming is risky also because a horse can incur a catastrophic injury during the race. If you have made a successful claim, once the starting gate opens, you own that horse. Unless you have arranged for insurance ahead of time, a catastrophic injury that results in euthanasia would mean a total loss of the money you put up.

Why does anyone take the risk of claiming a filly or mare as a broodmare prospect? To get a bargain. Just be sure you understand the potential risk.

Insurance & Transportation

Insurance

At an auction the buyer assumes the risk of ownership the moment the hammer falls. That's why the equine mortality insurance you can arrange for beforehand is called fall of the hammer coverage. It takes effect immediately upon transfer of ownership and covers you for loss of your investment in case of fatal injury, however soon it might occur.

If you plan to buy at auction, you can contact an equine insurance agent and provide the name that you or your representative will use to sign the ticket. You need not provide a hip number. A blanket statement requesting fall of the hammer coverage is all that is required, and coverage will apply to any horses purchased at the sale.

It costs nothing to arrange for fall of the hammer coverage if you wind up not buying any horses. You pay only if you buy a horse. The premium rate you pay depends upon the age, purchase price, and use of the horse. Broodmares up to age 14 would be insured at 3.25 percent, but after age 14 the premium rate for broodmares increases with each year of age.

You can get insurance before you claim a horse, too with a phone call to an equine insurance agent stating the specifics about the prospective claim. If you are successful in getting the horse, your claiming insurance will convert into an equine mortality insurance policy on that horse after the race. No premium is owed if the would-be claimant is not successful.

The purpose of insurance is to protect your investment. At the time of purchase, the investment would be the purchase price plus the agent's commission, plus initial transportation costs, and even the cost of the insurance. On average, 10 percent can be added onto the purchase price to include all of these expenditures.

An equine mortality insurance policy is a fair market value policy. The purchase price sets the initial value. However, the value of a horse can change from one day to the next. In the case of a broodmare, it can increase considerably if one of her older offspring wins a graded stakes race after you buy her.

Be aware that your insurance coverage will not automatically adjust if an older offspring wins a major race. You, as the insured, will have to contact the insurance company with a request to adjust the coverage for a higher value (although sometimes, alert insurance companies will contact the

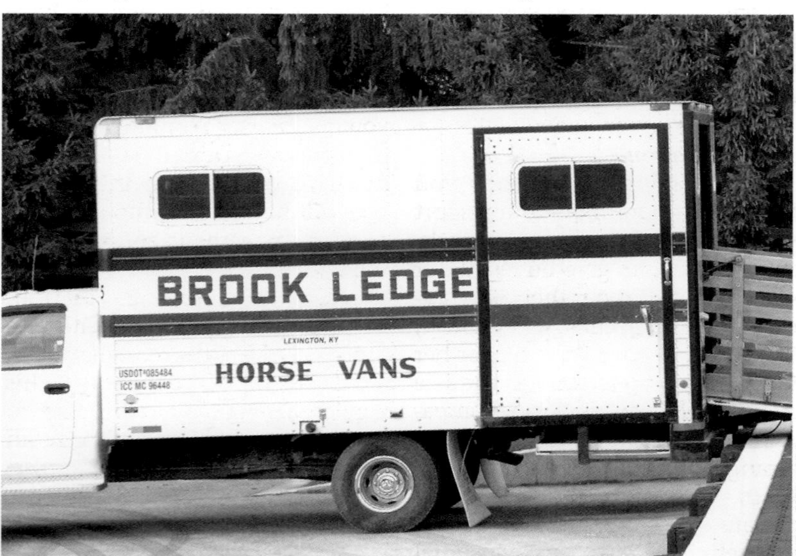

ANNE M. EBERHARDT

Be sure to arrange transportation for your new mare

insured to advise them that they might want to adjust for a higher value). Alternatively, if a broodmare is demonstrating that she is not a good-quality producer, the insurance company will want to adjust down; insurance companies do not want to be in a situation in which the horse is over-insured and therefore worth more dead than alive. The insurance company can advise you if it is time to reassess in a letter accompanying the annual policy expiration notice.

When you discuss with other breeders the question of insuring your mare, you might be surprised to learn that not every breeder insures every mare that he or she owns. A breeder with a large number of mares might only insure a few. Many breeders say it is simply too expensive to insure all of their mares, and that owning several mares spreads the risk. You can purchase insurance when buying your first mare; then after you gain experience and expand your operation, you might reassess whether you feel comfortable assuming risk on every mare.

Transportation

After buying at auction, you have the responsibility to transport your mare off the sales grounds. Sales companies give buyers 24 or 48 hours to ship out their purchases, but for the welfare of the mare, it is better to have arranged for her to be picked up as soon as the sale is final. Commercial van companies have agents at the sales and arrangements can be made with them. Or, you might invest in a private trailer and take her home yourself. Sales company personnel will ask to see the stable release form issued by the sales office before letting the horse load.

THINGS TO KNOW

Finding an Agent

In an effort to help attract and retain new owners, several leading industry organizations created "The Greatest Game, Inc." in 2003. The program matches new buyers with consultants approved by The Greatest Game committee. Approved consultants must adhere to a strict code of ethics. For more information, contact the Thoroughbred Owners and Breeders Association at (859) 276-2291 or visit www.thegreatestgame.com.

How To Buy

By yourself or through an agent

It takes confidence to sally forth and buy mares on your own. This can be especially true against the backdrop of a public auction, where bidding against other would-be buyers can be somewhat intimidating. If you already have some experience in the industry, know some of the people, and know conformation and pedigrees, you might feel confident enough to represent yourself in buying a mare. At an auction, this means you will be the one who signs the purchase agreement, also known as the sales slip.

Before attending an auction, make sure you register with the office so the sales company can check your credit history. This applies whether you are going to represent yourself or authorize an agent to represent you.

Newcomers to the industry are often advised to hire an adviser or agent who can give them the benefit of knowledge and experience.

In the same breath, the breeding neophytes are warned to watch out for "unscrupulous characters" conducting business as agents. Bloodstock agents are paid a commission to buy and sell horses. They may also give advice on pedigrees, breeding, and racing, and some also consign horses to sales. It was mentioned earlier that agents are one source through which you can find a mare for sale privately. Reputable agents should disclose when they are also representing the seller of a mare they are advising you to purchase. This is now mandated by law in Kentucky.

It is wise to interview several agents before choosing one to represent you. A few sources to call for the names of reputable agents are the state breeder associations, the sales companies, and breeding farm managers.

You can also contact The Greatest Game Inc., a partnership of the National Thoroughbred Racing Association (NTRA), Thoroughbred Owners and Breeders Association (TOBA), Keeneland Association, and *The Blood-Horse* magazine. The Greatest Game's consultant program matches new buyers with consultants — i.e., agents — who have been "vetted" by The Greatest Game committee. The approved consultants agree to adhere to a code of ethics that encompasses key issues such as principal's control and consent, commissions and fees, disclosure of conflicts of interest, and competent representation, which requires the agent have a substantial knowledge of the Thoroughbred industry, its customs, and its trade practices.

In order to have an agent represent you at auction, you must fill out and sign a buyer's authorized agent form, appointing someone to sign a purchase

ANNE M. EBERHARDT

Have a plan for housing your mare and resulting foals

agreement on your behalf.

The standard bloodstock agent fee is a 5 percent commission based on the purchase price.

Sole ownership or partnership

Sole ownership means you are in control, making decisions such as which stallion to breed your mare to and whether to sell or keep the offspring. You are also the only one putting up all of the money to purchase the mare and pay her expenses.

In a partnership, you share the cost of ownership with the other partners, each of whom buys a share in a mare. Usually, there is a general manager, or controlling partner, who makes the final decisions. Some partnerships are formed when people who know one another decide to become partners. Other partnerships are created as investment opportunities in which partners are solicited through advertisements. You can insure your share in a partnership even when other partners do not insure their shares.

Housing Your Mare

Hands-on operation

The ultimate dream for many of us who love horses is to be able to look out the window of our house on our farm and see our mare stretch into a carefree canter across a verdant paddock; tail raised high, wind in her mane, and a fine, healthy foal at her side.

Perhaps you already own property large enough for you to keep your mare in a hands-on operation. Or, perhaps buying a farm is part of the plan.

The most important thing a person needs in order to take care of his or her own mare and foal is experience working with horses. Even a little experience is helpful to start out; the longer you work with horses, the more experience you will acquire. Studying from books and videos and talking to people who have worked with horses will supplement what you learn from your day-to-day experiences.

Before bringing your mare to your property, be sure professional veterinary and farrier services are in the area. Have an emergency plan for anything that could go wrong. It is always a good idea to have your horse trailer hooked up and ready to go. A working horse farm requires a lot of maintenance. That translates into labor and money. In addition to the investment in land and structures, other aspects of farm ownership include:

- pasture management
- manure disposal
- ensuring sufficient water
- maintaining fencing

Boarding

Another option is to board your mare at a farm that provides foaling and other services and bills you, the breeder. Boarding costs vary by region, and a variety of services might be included in the day rate. Services not included in the day rate are billed separately to the breeder. Ask what services will be separate charges. Some farms charge a small additional fee for care of a suckling foal. Most farms charge a separate foaling fee.

But there is more to finding the right boarding farm for your mare than cost. You want assurance that your mare and foal will be happy and thrive in their surroundings. For yourself, you need to be compatible with the farm staff. Ideally, you will develop a permanent relationship with the farm. Just as you did prior to buying your mare and choosing an agent or adviser, you will have to do your homework in choosing a boarding farm. It's important to consider:

- the farm's reputation
- the appearance of barn, stalls, and pastures
- the appearance of the horses
- population of the paddocks
- available veterinary care — resident veterinarian vs. the services of a full-time vet
- the experience of the staff

Whatever housing option you choose, make sure your mares receive the best possible care and management. And hopefully you'll have a healthy foal on the ground come spring. *By Bettina Cohen*

PART II

Planning a Mating

Selecting a Stallion

Someone can't set out to breed a Seattle Slew, Billy Turner, trainer of the Triple Crown great, once said. "They just show up."

As Turner so eloquently points out: The role of chance can't be underplayed when it comes to breeding a legend such as Seattle Slew or even when it comes to breeding a winner. But there are some steps mare owners can take that might tilt the odds a little more in their favor.

First, novice breeders should seek guidance, and, second, they should educate themselves on the subject of stallion selection as much as possible. In addition, they should use the same common sense they would in starting a business, including devising a financial plan.

Be Realistic

Most mare owners do not have a limitless bankroll. The adage "Breed the best to the best and hope for the best" is not within the realm of their finances. A plan will help new breeders selecting a stallion keep within their monetary parameters, help them remain in the horse business at a level at which they are financially comfortable, and help them set realistic goals.

"You can't make a silk purse out of a sow's ear," says industry analyst Bill Oppenheim. "It's great to love your mare, but make sure you see what you really have and work with that. If you have realistic expectations, you'll be disappointed far less and enjoy being a breeder far more."

The worth of the mare is integral when you are selecting a stallion, particularly if the offspring is headed for the auction ring.

"As a rule of thumb, if you get outside a range of one-quarter to one-third of the value of your broodmare for your stud fee, you are probably over- or under-breeding her, and you may be disappointed in the auction price you receive for the resulting foal," said Arnold Kirkpatrick, author of *Investing in Thoroughbreds* (Eclipse Press, 2001).

This guideline will help novice mare owners hone in on stallions with stud fees in the recommended financial strata. For example, if a mare is worth $24,000, her owner should seek a stallion with a stud fee ranging between $6,000 and $8,000. Any stallion outside that range would be considered under- or over-breeding and would not be advisable, particularly if the offspring is headed to auction.

Also, keep in mind the additional cost of transporting a mare to be bred or boarding a mare to be bred to a stallion that stands out of the area.

Get Advice and Get Educated

While the math on how much to spend on a stud fee is simple, the selection of the best-suited stallion, within that range, is not. Two important considerations are conformation/performance and pedigree — and they are not easy subjects. *(See Chapters 5 and 6.)*

Theories abound on both, and countless books, indices, and articles address the strengths and weaknesses of Thoroughbred family lines and which cross well together. This is where an adviser, such as a reputable farm manager or bloodstock agent, is beneficial. A bloodstock agent's job is to know pedigree and conformation the way an English teacher knows grammar and punctuation. A local and reputable farm manager can also help steer you in the right direction, though not with the same enthusiasm and detail of someone who is getting paid for his or her knowledge.

Oppenheim said he always recommends to newcomers that they seek paid professional advice.

"Unless you are a 'stockman' yourself, don't forget we're dealing with livestock here," he said. "There is a tremendous range of people who really are experts, both with horses and in the business. It's great to be able to make the decisions yourself — that's part of the fun of it, after all — but I find that the people who get advice from the experts make better decisions."

As Oppenheim says, part of the fun is for owners to participate in important decisions, so mare owners should educate themselves to the level at which they can comfortably participate in selecting the right stallions for their mares.

When selecting a stallion, Oppenheim also advises not making a distinction between breeding to race and breeding to sell, even though some breeders tend to do so.

"You're always breeding to race, no matter what," he said. "Usually, these days, you're breeding to sell, too. Fortunately, there's a high correlation between what runs and what sells. I always cringe when I hear somebody say they don't care if it runs or not, they're just trying to make money. There must be a better way to make money, if that's all you're trying to do."

One endeavor a novice mare owner can easily undertake is studying the performance records of the stallions being considered. Research how many starts a stallion had and against what kind of company and where. Talk to the owner, trainer, and jockey about the horse, if possible.

Contacting the prior connections can also be fruitful for a novice breeder who has purchased an older mare. The previous owners may be able to pass along some of the common strengths and weaknesses found in the mare's previous foals. The power of a phone call cannot be overstated when it comes to successfully managing a broodmare's career.

No Perfect Stallion

Remember, every stallion, or horse for that matter, has some physical fault with regard to conformation. The art or science of evaluating a stallion is deciding which of those faults are less likely to impact the offspring adversely. It is helpful to know something about the pedigree of the horse as it may relate to a particular horse's conformation. Some sires pass similar conformational faults to offspring, with some of the faults having little or no consequence with respect to racing success.

"Pretty is as pretty does," Three Chimneys Farm president Dan Rosenberg told participants about conformation at a breeding stock selection seminar a few years ago.

Rosenberg downplayed minor conformation flaws in stallions. If a horse can sire runners, he said, buyers tend to forgive conformation flaws that they expect to see by that sire.

For example, Storm Cat is known for having some offspring with offset knees. When Storm Cat first went to stud, in 1988, Overbrook Farm charged $30,000 a season. When buyers saw some of his less-than-correct progeny, his stud fee dropped as low as $25,000 in 1991. It wasn't until his first babies hit the track and began running like the wind that Storm Cat's stud fee began a meteoric rise. In 2006 he commanded a $500,000 stud fee.

Proven Stallions

Breeding a young mare to a proven sire also will give a mare owner greater odds of a good outcome.

"I find, in general, that young mares are bred to proven stallions to get them off to a good start, and older mares are bred to unproven stallions to get the stallions off to a good start," Rosenberg said. "Since most unproven stallions don't make the grade, younger mares have a far greater opportunity to come up with a good racehorse than older mares."

A proven stallion also provides other progeny against which to measure a mare's first offspring and, hence, what the mare can get.

"For a mare's first mating, I try to breed to a proven sire with at least a little speed," Oppenheim said. "Commercially, it's a good idea to try and kick a mare off with an early

ANNE M. EBERHARDT

Inspect a potential stallion's conformation

ANNE M. EBERHARDT

Breeding to a proven stallion can boost a mare's sales potential

winner, and if you use a proven sire, you or your advisers will have an idea what that horse usually throws. That gives you a basis for comparison with your mare."

Also, he advises, if an owner plans to keep a mare longer than one breeding season, try to devise a rotation to start with, rather than just pick a single stallion each year.

"You might have a mare who appears to be equally well suited, let's say, by sires from the Danzig line and from the Seattle Slew line," Oppenheim said. "I would send her to one the first year and the other the second year.

"The advantage of this is that you can then sometimes tell whether a mare seems to do better with one line or the other, or if she's indifferent in that respect (for example, if she dominates the stallion); in the medium to longer term, this should work to your advantage."

When selecting a stallion, consider the number of offspring the stallion already has.

The stallion should have enough foals on the racetrack to give him an opportunity to show his prowess as a sire.

"With stallions that have very small books, you are fighting an uphill battle as a breeder," Rosenberg said.

On the flip side, breeders should also keep in mind how much competition they will have selling the weanlings or yearlings of a popular stallion with a very large book.

Genetics

In planning matings, many experts advise breeding strength to strength and avoiding breeding weakness to weakness. This pertains not only to conformation traits but also to racing characteristics and temperament.

Some breeders try and compensate for a horse's characteristic by breeding the horse to a horse with the opposite characteristic.

"I remember in high school biology learning about Gregor Mendel, the father of genetics," Rosenberg said. "He bred tall peas to short peas, and he didn't get any medium peas. You either get tall or short; that's the way genetics work.

"But I find people who have a great big mare and breed her to a tiny horse thinking they are going to get an average-sized foal, or they've got this tiny mare and want to breed her to a stallion seventeen hands to breed some size into her. I don't find it works that way at all.

"The same with speed and stamina. You have a mare that was really quick at five furlongs and breed her to a horse that could run a mile and a half, and you think you will get a horse that can run a mile. I think that what you get is something that can't run at all."

Mating two horses with similar conformation characteristics will produce more consistent conformation results, he said.

"You have a mare that is presumably a model of what you are trying to accomplish. If you breed her to a widely divergent type of horse, sometimes you are going to get what he looks like, sometimes you are going to get what she looks like. It's always a guessing game and the odds are always against you, but if you breed like to like, you narrow that range and are more likely to get what you are looking for."

State-bred Incentive Programs

Many states have devised incentive programs for breeders. These programs help fill fields at local racetracks, give the Thoroughbred industry clout in the state legislature, preserve green space, and contribute to a state's economy. Mare owners should become familiar with their state's program so as not to miss out on opportunities for additional income.

Each state's criteria for these incentive programs vary. For example, eligibility for bonuses in Kentucky requires a horse be sired by a stallion standing in the state for the entire season in which the horse was conceived and for the horse to be foaled in the state. Eligibility in Louisiana requires a foal be produced from a mare that permanently resides in the state. The mare may, after foaling, be shipped out of state to be bred, provided she is returned to Louisiana no later than August 1.

Rules and regulations often change so mare owners need to be sure to keep up to date on their state's program.

For information on state-bred incentive programs, contact the Thoroughbred Owners and Breeders Association on the Web at www.toba.org or call (859) 276-2291.

Rosenberg said that rarely is a stallion's influence strong enough to overcome and improve on the mare to whom he is bred.

Oppenheim cautions against breeding extreme types to extreme types.

"This almost never works: we're trying to breed horses here, not elephants or rats," he said. "But I really am talking extremes — seventeen hands to seventeen hands or fifteen hands to fifteen hands."

Breaking the Rules

Though breeders develop certain philosophies, rarely are they absolute. Meadowlark Valley Farm owner and commercial breeder Marvin Little Jr. told *The Blood-Horse* in a 2006 interview that he broke one of his cardinal rules in the breeding of Hansel, who won the 1991 Preakness and Belmont stakes and was named champion three-year-old colt. Little got Hansel by breeding an unproven mare, Count On Bonnie, to an unproven stallion at the time, Woodman.

"You should never do that, but sometimes you end up breaking the rules," Little said. "In this case it worked. Sometimes you have to do what your pocketbook calls for."

A key for him, Little said, is to catch stallions on the way up and also support then in the crucial third and fourth years when others may not.

"I bred to Giant's Causeway when he was $60,000 (now $300,000), Fusaichi Pegasus for $70,000 ($125,000), Northern Afleet for $3,500 ($20,000), and Bernstein for $5,000 ($25,000)," Little told *The Blood-Horse*. "I caught all of those on the way up."

Rosenberg aptly advises: "Always buy as much pedigree, as much performance, and as good conformation as you can afford."

In the End

In the end, no matter how careful and selective a breeder is, the odds are against making a profit in the marketplace or making the grade on the racetrack.

"We just hope that one day we can breed one or sell one or race one that makes up for all the others," Rosenberg concluded. "But this is a wonderful challenge. It is a great combination of art and science. You have to control all the factors you can, and in the end, you just go with your gut feeling and hope you have guessed right enough of the time to get a little bit lucky.

"You have to love this to do it. You have to be at least half crazy, and probably all the way crazy helps, to persevere."

By Rena Baer

Breeding Contracts

The excitement of planning a mating and anticipation of the resulting foal should never overshadow good common sense when it comes to signing a breeding contract. Mare owners, or someone trustworthy who is representing their interest — such as an attorney, bloodstock agent, or farm manager — should go over every line of the contract and make sure all the conditions and stipulations are well understood.

Even a mare owner working with a representative should know exactly what it is he or she is signing. In fact, it may be helpful for mare owners to request a "for information only" copy of the breeding contracts of stallions they are considering for their mares. This way, mare owners have all the conditions before they decide which stallion to breed their mare to.

"You need to read the contract thoroughly and understand all clauses," said Catherine Parke, owner of Valkyre Stud, a Thoroughbred farm in Lexington, Kentucky, that manages and boards broodmares. "You need to ask for an explanation on anything you don't understand."

Most mare owners try and have their breeding contracts in order by January at the very latest (the breeding season begins in mid-February). Many good stallions are already booked by the time the Keeneland November breeding stock sale begins early in the month.

Parke said that new owners who want to breed their mares should seek some help from reputable professionals in the industry. "If you are dealing with a good farm manager, talk to them first," she said. "It's hard for someone new in the business to pick up the phone and start negotiating deals. It's important to have someone who can tell you who's reputable, who's fertile, who's overpriced, and what's realistic — it's like when I'm looking for stocks to buy, I go to a stockbroker. There's quite a bit of expertise involved in this."

Before doing so, it is still helpful to understand the basics of a breeding contract. No one has more at stake in this negotiation than the mare owner, and a knowledgeable mare owner is in a much better position to look out for his or her own interests in the process.

Breeding Contract Basics

Most contracts are provided by the stallion owner or a bloodstock agent and are fairly standard. The variances are usually the stud fee, its due date, and the type of contract.

The three primary types of contracts are the following:

- live foal guarantee
- in foal guarantee
- no guarantee

For decades many live foal guarantee contracts made the stud fee payable when the foal stood and nursed. As stallion owners gained the upper hand in dictating the terms, this type of arrangement fell out of vogue. Most contracts began requiring that the stud fee be paid by late summer, early fall — often September 1 — if the mare was pregnant. (Most mares are covered once per heat cycle during the breeding season until they get into foal. Some are vanned in each time, and others, such as a Florida-based mare being bred to a Kentucky stallion, might be boarded temporarily. These boarding terms also may be included in the breeding contract.)

If the mare does not get in foal or aborts before the stud fee is due, a veterinarian must sign a certificate attesting that she isn't pregnant. This certificate must be presented to the stallion owner or manager to release the mare owner from paying the stud fee.

If the contract stipulates a live foal guarantee and the mare loses the foal after the stud fee is paid or the foal is stillborn or it cannot stand on its own and nurse, the owner must again provide a veterinarian's certificate to receive a refund. (Depending on the contract, the owner of a mare that does not produce a live or healthy foal might be entitled to a return breeding to the stallion at no cost rather than a refund of the stud fee.)

Gray areas do pop up, said Parke, such as a foal being born sick and requiring veterinary assistance to stand and nurse or the foal being able to stand and nurse but still being very sickly and unable to pass a subsequent health exam required to get it insured. The best course of action is to call the stallion farm immediately and communicate openly and honestly. The last thing an owner wants is to be out a foal, a stud fee, and have a big vet bill to boot, Parke said.

"Farms are usually willing to work something out on the fee if you contact them immediately and let them know what is going on," Parke said.

According to attorney Milton Toby, of Lexington, Kentucky, co-author of *Understanding Equine Law* (Eclipse Press, 1999), if a breeding contract simply makes payment of the stud fee contingent on a live foal, with no other explanation, the mare owner should insist that "live foal" be defined to his or her satisfaction and that the payment schedule be set out in detail.

A variation on the live foal agreement is a "guaranteed in foal" contract. With this type of agreement, the stallion owner assumes the risk of the mare getting in foal, but the mare owner is responsible for the full stud fee if the mare is in foal at some specified time after she is last bred to the stallion (typically 45 to 60 days). If the mare loses her foal after that date or fails to produce a live foal, the stallion owner is not obligated to refund the stud fee. In this case, a veterinarian's certificate confirming that the mare was not in foal by the date specified is necessary to avoid responsibility for the stud fee.

Another variation, and a less common one, is a no guarantee contract. With this type of agreement, the mare owner takes all the risk. The stud fee is paid and is not refundable, regardless of whether the mare conceives. No guarantee contracts are more common among proven and popular stallions, whose owners can call the shots when negotiating with mare owners.

Mare owners can protect themselves in this case by purchasing barrenness/conception insurance, which guarantees a mare will conceive and produce a single live foal and that the foal will survive its first 30 days or longer, depending

STALLION SERVICE CONTRACT

THIS STALLION SERVICE CONTRACT, made and entered into this ____ day of __________, 2006, by and between the SELLER, the owner of a 2006 _____ (regular or bonus) season (the "Season") from share #______ to the thoroughbred stallion _______________ (the "Stallion") and the PURCHASER.

<u>SELLER</u> <u>PURCHASER</u>

1. Seller hereby sells, transfers and assigns to Purchaser and Purchaser hereby purchases from Seller the Season on which Season Purchaser agrees to breed the thoroughbred mare __________________ (the "Mare") to the Stallion. The purchase price hereunder shall be $_____________ Dollars ($____________ stud fee + $__________ Kentucky sales tax payable to ___________), due and payable on or before **September 1,** of the year bred, unless the Mare is not pregnant, in which case Purchaser shall deliver to Seller a veterinary certificate to that effect in lieu of the purchase price. In the event Purchaser's payment, or any portion thereof, is more than forty five (45) days past due, all live foal warranties provided herein shall be cancelled and extinguished ab initio. This agreement shall thereafter be construed as a no guarantee stallion service contract and the purchase price hereunder shall be due, payable and non-refundable for any reason whatsoever related to the Mare and her foal in utero. Seller makes <u>NO REPRESENTATIONS OR WARRANTIES, EXPRESS OR IMPLIED, OF MERCHANTABILITY, FITNESS FOR A PARTICULAR PURPOSE, SUITABILITY, BREEDING SOUNDNESS, OR FERTILITY OF THE STALLION OR HIS SEMEN.</u> All past due amounts shall further bear interest at the rate of one and one-half percent (1-1/2%) per month (18% per annum), or at the highest rate allowed by law, whichever shall be less.

2. Except as provided in Paragraph 1, Seller hereby agrees that in the event he has received payment and the Mare does not produce a single live foal that can stand alone and nurse as a result of said breeding, Seller shall refund the fee of $_________ (including sales tax) without interest to Purchaser, provided that Purchaser furnishes a satisfactory veterinary certificate to that effect within twenty one (21) days of the date the Mare foals, aborts or dies. Seller shall refund to Purchaser the aforesaid amount within thirty (30) days of receiving such certificate. In the event the Mare produces twins and Purchaser shall desire to register one or both of said twins, then the purchase price provided hereunder shall be due, payable, and non-refundable notwithstanding the provisions of this Paragraph 2.

3. Purchaser agrees that the Mare shall be healthy and in sound breeding condition. Purchaser further acknowledges that the breeding of the Mare shall be subject to the customary rules and procedures of the Stallion Manager and may obligate Purchaser to present a veterinary certificate with respect to the health and breeding condition of the Mare. In the event the Mare, prior to being covered one (1) time by the Stallion, becomes unfit or unable to breed, or is refused by the Stallion Manager to be bred, Purchaser shall furnish a satisfactory veterinary certificate specifying the reason for the Mare's unavailability. Purchaser may nominate another mare to the Stallion and this Agreement shall apply as if the substitute Mare were the original Mare named herein. If Purchaser shall fail (a) to nominate a substitute Mare within seven (7) days from when he knew or should have known of the original Mare's unavailability, or (b) to present the original Mare for any reason other than those specified above, or (c) to present the substitute mare for any reason whatsoever, or (d) to supply appropriate documentation as specified above, or (e) if the Purchaser shall breed the Mare or substitute mare to any other Stallion during the breeding season, then, in any of such events, the purchase price hereunder shall be immediately due, payable and non-refundable, shall be conclusively considered earned by Seller and/or shall serve as liquidated damages to Seller, and all live foal warranties shall be cancelled and extinguished.

4. Seller shall have the right to approve the substitute mare nominated pursuant to Paragraph 3 above. In the event Seller shall refuse to approve any such substitute mare, or in the event the Stallion should die, be sold, or become unfit for breeding prior to servicing the Mare, then this Agreement shall be null and void.

5. This Agreement shall not be assigned or transferred without the prior written consent of Seller, which consent may be withheld for any reason whatsoever. In the event the Mare is sold, catalogued for sale (whether or not such sale is completed), otherwise transferred, or transported out of the continental United States, the purchase price hereunder shall be immediately due and payable, if not previously paid, and shall be non-refundable under any circumstances.

6. The parties further agree that neither party shall be liable or responsible to the other for any disease, accident or injury to the Stallion or to the Mare.

7. Seller warrants that Purchaser will receive clear and unencumbered title to the season.

8. In order to secure payment of the purchase price hereunder, Purchaser hereby grants to Seller and Seller hereby retains a security interest in and to the foal to be produced, the stallion service certificate applicable to said foal. Pursuant thereto, Seller, or the Stallion Manager as his agent, shall be permitted to retain the said stallion service certificate until all obligations of Purchaser to Seller hereunder are performed in full. Purchaser further appoints Seller, or his designee, as Purchaser's attorney-in-fact for the purpose of executing on Purchaser's behalf and filing such financing statements (UCC-1 or equivalent) as Seller may deem appropriate covering Purchaser's interest in said foal, the stallion service contract, and any and all registration papers applicable to the foal.

9. This Agreement shall be binding upon and insure to the benefit of the parties hereto, their personal representatives, heirs, successors, and permitted assigns and shall be governed by and construed in accordance with laws of the Commonwealth of Kentucky. The parties acknowledge that this Agreement contains the entire agreement of the parties, and each party represents to the other that he is not relying upon any verbal assurance of any nature whatsoever that is not contained or expressed herein. The parties further agree that time is of the essence in the performance of the rights and duties hereunder. In the event litigation is commenced with respect to any dispute arising from this Agreement the prevailing party shall be entitled to recover its costs and expenses thereof, including its reasonable attorneys' fees, from the non-prevailing party.

10. In the event an agent executes this Agreement on behalf of this principal, such agent affirmatively represents and warrants that he is duly authorized to enter into this Agreement for and on behalf of his principal.

11. This Agreement may be executed with counterpart signatures, all of which taken together shall constitute an original without the necessity of all parties signing each document. This Agreement may also be executed by signatures to fax or telecopy documents in lieu of original or machine generated or copied documents.

IN WITNESS WHEREOF, the parties have caused this Agreement to be executed in duplicate as of the date set forth opposite their respective names.

SELLER	PURCHASER
DATE	DATE
FEDERAL IDENTIFICATION OR SOCIAL SECURITY NUMBER	FEDERAL IDENTIFICATION OR SOCIAL SECURITY NUMBER

A typical breeding contract (not actual size)

ANNE M. EBERHARDT

Explore your contract options when choosing a stallion

on the particular policy. These policies usually run between 21 percent and 26 percent of the stud fee, so if a mare owner is paying a $40,000 stud fee, he or she can count on paying between $8,400 and $10,400 for barrenness/conception insurance. This type of insurance is unnecessary with a live foal guarantee, which serves as its own insurance.

Sometimes both no guarantee and live foal guarantee contracts will be available for less popular stallions as well. Generally, fees that are not guaranteed are discounted to account for the risk that is shifted from the stallion owner to the mare owner. Buying insurance to guarantee the mare will get in foal and produce a live, healthy foal only makes financial sense if the cost of the insurance is less than the money saved by getting the no guarantee season. In other words, if a stallion stands for $25,000 guaranteed and for $20,000 not guaranteed, the mare owner will come out behind if he or she pays $6,000 for insurance that will compensate if no healthy foal materializes.

A few breeding contracts, mainly those negotiated by bloodstock agents who manage stallion syndicates, split the responsibility, designating part of the stud fee as non-refundable while making the remaining portion contingent on the production of a live foal.

Kentucky equine attorney Mike Meuser said he is seeing the pendulum swing back to stand and nurse contracts.

"It used to be that every payment was due September 1," he said. "Now there are a lot more stand and nurse contracts. It is due to competition among the farms."

He said he's also seeing more mare owners and stallion owners negotiate more complicated or riskier arrangements.

"A lot of people are doing out-of-proceeds deals," he said. "For out-of-proceeds agreements, you bring the mare in to breed to my stallion, we agree she is going to sell in the fall, and the stallion owner gets the first $15,000 off the top (to cover a $15,000 stud fee).

"A few people are doing deals where the fee is paid after the foal sells. Mare sharing has been around for a couple years, but it is getting more popular. We might be looking at putting a $15,000 stud fee into a mare that may be worth $10,000 if she were barren, but could be worth $60,000 if she is in foal to a first- or second-year stallion. So the stallion owner and the mare owner both roll the dice. A straight mare share is 50-50. The stallion owner puts up the stud fee and the mare owner brings the mare, and they split whatever she brings at the sale."

Loss of Live Foal Guarantee

Make sure to be aware of circumstances that could nullify or change a live foal guarantee. For example, if the stud fee is not paid when due, the contract may stipulate that after 30 days of non-payment, the contract becomes no guarantee. Or the contract may come with no grace period. A mare owner must assume the stallion owner plans to enforce the contract as written and should not sign it unless he or she fully intends to abide by the provisions.

The sale of the mare also usually means the stud fee is due immediately and the live foal guarantee is no longer in effect. Some contracts go as far as stipulating that merely entering a mare in a sale will make the stud fee due immediately and will void the live foal guarantee.

As said at the beginning of this chapter, mare owners should request a contract "for information only" on each stallion seriously being considered. This way the contract can be studied carefully and provisions that concern the mare owner possibly can be negotiated.

"Mare owners need to read these contracts carefully and if there is something that does not make sense or does not seem like a fair allocation of risk they should ask," Meuser said. "You know, they get these pre-printed contracts that seem set in stone, but farm owners are usually willing to make some changes."

Stallion and Mare Health

Any mare sent to a stallion must be in sound breeding condition. The contract may require that a veterinarian's certificate accompany the mare to the breeding shed. An information sheet containing the horse's health and breeding history, vaccination schedules, and other background information may also be necessary.

Contracts usually allow the stallion manager or owner to refuse to breed any mare if the breeding would endanger the health or welfare of the stallion. This provision can include vicious or unmanageable mares, as well as unhealthy mares.

On the flip side, a variety of circumstances can make it impossible for a stallion owner or manager to fulfill the contract. The stallion might have died, been injured, or become too ill to breed. He might have become infertile, or health problems might have forced the stallion manager to cut down the number of mares to which the stallion breeds.

Under these types of circumstances, most breeding contracts

THINGS TO KNOW

Live foal guarantee — Stud fee is returned or, if not yet paid, is void if the mare does not get pregnant, aborts, or delivers a sickly foal that cannot stand and nurse. Sometimes the stud fee is due in the fall of the pregnancy and sometimes it is due when the foal stands and nurses.

In foal guarantee — Stud fee is due on predetermined date and is not returnable once the mare is pregnant.

No guarantee — Mare owner assumes all the risk and must pay the stud fee regardless of whether the mare gets pregnant.

ANNE M. EBERHARDT

Some stud fees are payable when the foal stands and nurses

become null and void, and neither the stallion manager nor the mare owner has any obligation to the other, though some contracts give the mare owner access to another stallion, if feasible.

If the mare gets sick or dies before she is bred to a stallion the first time in a season, some contracts may allow another mare to be substituted. If the mare has already been bred once, her owners are generally prohibited from substituting another mare. If the contract allows another mare to be substituted, a veterinarian's certificate stating the original mare cannot be bred is required.

Security Agreement

Almost all contracts contain a security agreement that provides the stallion owner or manager a way to force payment of the stud fee if the mare owner doesn't fulfill his or her obligation. Signing a contract with such a provision transfers a security interest in the mare, in the resulting foal, and in the foal's registration documents to the stallion manager or owner. Many contracts also allow the stallion owner to retain the breeding certificate until the stud fee is paid. By keeping a security interest in the mare and foal, and in the foal's registration papers, the stallion owner can repossess and sell the mare and foal, if necessary to pay the bill. Also, without a breeding certificate, the mare owner will likely be unable to register the foal.

Other Provisions

The following provisions, according to Toby, also are likely to be found in a typical breeding contract:

• Complete identification of the stallion, mare, mare owner, and stallion manager or owner, and farm where the stallion stands;

• Addresses and emergency contact numbers for all the parties involved in the contract;

• A statement that the stallion owner or manager has a good and marketable title to the season being sold, and that there are no liens on the season;

• Waivers of liability for the stallion owner or manager and the owner of the farm where the stallion stands in the event the mare is injured;

• The earliest and latest dates on which a mare can be bred;

• Estimated expenses for board, veterinary care, farrier service, and other costs if the mare will be boarded at the farm where the stallion stands; and,

• In states where it is required by law that limits a farm owner's liability, a notice about inherent risks in equine activities.

The best protection a mare owner can have is making sure he or she understands the contract before signing it. *By Rena Baer*

Conformation

Conformation is one of the key components in planning a mating. Your goal should be to breed as sound a horse as possible. To that end, is the potential dam a well-made individual? The potential sire? What flaws do they have? What strengths? If this mare and stallion were mated, would their strengths outweigh the flaws?

Genetics, of course, determine a horse's conformation. Each parent contributes 50 percent of its offspring's genetic material. Thus, as a breeder, you need to be cognizant of which body traits are more desirable and which should be avoided. Some horses can outrun bad conformation traits; however, that doesn't mean those horses should be bred because the bad traits can continue down the line. On the other hand, a poorly conformed stallion bred to a solid, sound mare has that 50 percent shot at siring a sound individual.

There are as many opinions about what constitutes good conformation as there are horsemen giving opinions. Some horsemen don't mind a horse that toes out while others wouldn't go near such an animal. Talk with your adviser about what he or she likes to see in a racehorse, which flaws are acceptable, and which are to be avoided if at all possible. Then go with your adviser to look at mares and stallions and have your adviser point out what's good or bad about each horse. That way you can develop your own eye for conformation.

A Balanced Individual

In evaluating conformation, don't discount your first impression of a horse. How does the horse look overall from all sides? Does it look like the front and hind ends fit together well? Is its body compact and muscular or tall and rangy? Does its neck fit its body? How does it carry its head? Is its back short or long and does it fit with the rest of the body? A horse that is well made is fairly obvious; as with a handsome man or a beautiful woman, you can see the horse looks good. By the same token, you can usually pick out a horse that isn't as attractive. That doesn't mean the horse can't run, just that it won't look as pretty in the winner's circle photos.

As you evaluate more and more horses, you will notice certain body types, such as the compact, more heavily muscled sprinter type and the leaner, rangier distance (stayer) or turf type. These body

THINGS TO KNOW

Do Your Homework!

- Analyze as many horses as you can to develop your eye for conformation — the horse's physical make-up.
- By developing your eye, you will begin to see characteristics imparted by certain sires and families.
- Many breeders seek to minimize or negate conformation flaws in one parent by breeding to a mate that does not possess those flaws.

types go hand in hand with pedigree: some bloodlines are known for perpetuating a certain type. As you examine horses physically, take note of their pedigree as well; you'll soon notice correlations between physical appearance and pedigree and be able to determine if a horse is "typey" for its bloodline. When the foal receives dominant traits from the sire, a sire is said to "stamp" his get when the offspring resembles the sire in body type and size and even color and markings Mares also can "stamp" their offspring but because mares produce only one foal a year to a stallion's dozens or hundreds, the trend is more evident with the stallion's offspring.

Once you've evaluated the horse as a whole, it's time to pay close attention to its legs and feet. A horse's legs and feet are the foun-

Biomechanical Matings

Biomechanics is defined as the study of the mechanics of a living body, especially of the forces exerted by muscles and gravity on the skeletal structure. As applied to racehorses, biomechanics studies a horse's efficiency of movement as an indicator of whether the animal has the potential to be a good racehorse. But biomechanics also can be used for planning matings.

ANNE M. EBERHARDT

Taking a mare's measurements

The Lexington, Kentucky-based Equix Biomechanics has a program called OptiMatch that matches a mare with compatible stallions and calculates the probable physical measurements and athletic ability of a foal from a proposed mating. To use this service, a mare owner contacts Equix to have the mare evaluated. An equine analyst comes to the barn (or wherever the mare is boarded) and takes 40 different body measurements of the mare, including angles of the shoulder, leg, and hip joints, the heart girth, the neck, etc. In addition, a visual examination is made of the mare's conformation to assess overall balance.

All of this information is plugged into the company's computer programs and run through the company's comprehensive stallion index. With stud fee range and location taken into consideration, the program provides potential matches based on structural compatibility between the mare and a particular stallion (or several stallions). Some mares will match with more stallions, providing breeders with more options.

Equix Biomechanics and other companies offering biomechanics services provide a useful tool for breeders looking for a little extra edge (or just plain help) in picking the right stallion. For more information about equine biomechanics, visit www.equixbio.com or check *The Blood-Horse Source* for other biomechanics companies.

dation, and you want to find a horse with a solid foundation.

Front-End Conformation

The front legs support up to 65 percent of a horse's weight and handle shock absorption, so good conformation in the front part of the body is important. If you are looking at a side view of an ideal Thoroughbred, the angle of the shoulder should be about 45 degrees, not straight and severe or too over-angled. To better understand the ideal conformation for the front leg, draw an imaginary line down the middle of the leg starting at the forearm, then moving through the knee, cannon bone, and fetlock (the ankle joint just above the pastern), and down to the ground. *(See illustration below.)* You can do the same thing with a head-on view, drawing that line down the center of the leg from the point of shoulder to the forearm through the knee, cannon bone, pastern, and the hoof to the ground. The bones and joints should align properly with no deviation from the imaginary mid-line. In addition, you will want to see good bone in the legs (both front and hind but especially in the front because of the increased concussion). Today's Thoroughbred has a more refined, lighter appearance compared to its ancestors of five or six generations ago, but you can still find horses with good bone — thicker, sturdier-looking legs (the cannon bones might be short but not always) underpinning a solid frame.

Of course, there's no such thing as a perfectly conformed horse. But that ideal example gives you a starting point when determining how much a horse's front legs

> **THINGS TO KNOW**
>
> **Points to Remember**
>
> - Each parent contributes 50 percent of an offspring's genetic material.
> - There is no such thing as a perfectly conformed horse.
> - Some horses will outrun their conformation flaws.

ROBIN PETERSON ILLUSTRATIONS

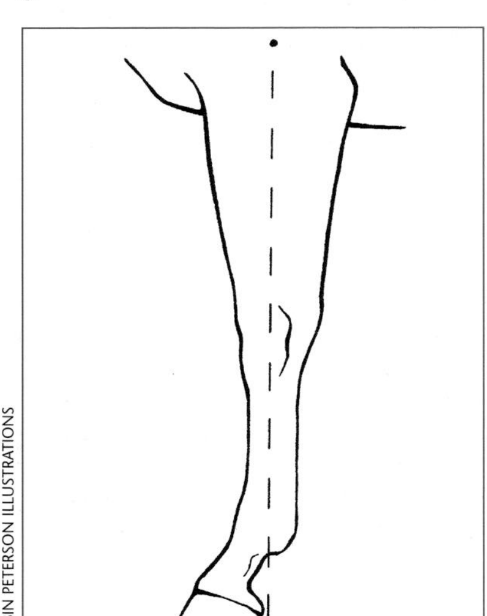

Ideal front leg conformation

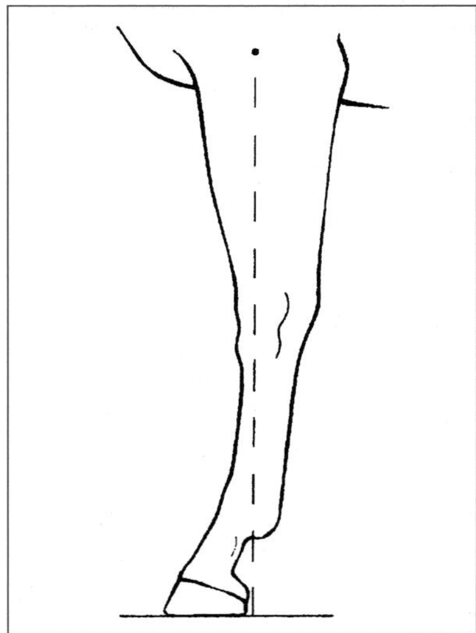

Back at the knee

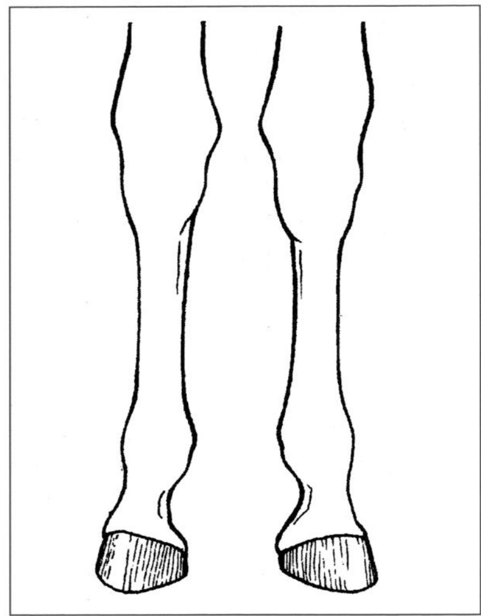

Toeing out

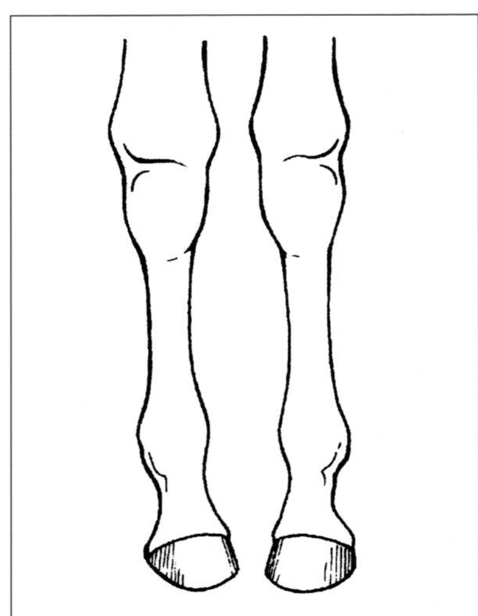
Toeing in

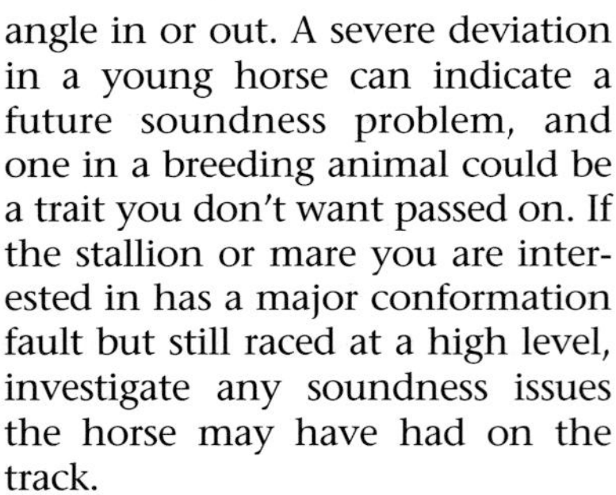
angle in or out. A severe deviation in a young horse can indicate a future soundness problem, and one in a breeding animal could be a trait you don't want passed on. If the stallion or mare you are interested in has a major conformation fault but still raced at a high level, investigate any soundness issues the horse may have had on the track.

Below are some of the main front leg conformation faults you will see in Thoroughbreds. For more about conformation, see the Resources section.

Toeing Out/Toeing In

Toeing out is considered a serious conformation defect. A horse toes out when its pasterns and hooves deviate outside the imaginary center line. When a horse toes out, its feet wing in as it walks. At racing speed, this can result in the horse striking the opposite leg as the motion becomes exaggerated. In addition, toeing out puts extra stress on the inside of the knee, which can result in splints or bony spurs on the cannon bone.

A horse that toes in (pigeon-toed) has a tendency to paddle and thus is not in danger of hitting itself as it moves. However, extra stress is still applied to the knees and the horse's stride may not be very efficient.

Offset Knees

Also called bench-knees, offset knees are another serious fault in which the forearm and cannon bone don't align and can lead to knee problems. As with toeing out and toeing in, you can observe this defect by viewing a horse head-on.

Back at the Knee/ Over at the Knee

When a horse is back at the knee *(See illustration on previous page.)* or calf-kneed, the knee joint lines up behind the imaginary center line, giving the leg a concave appearance when it is viewed from the side. This fault adds stress on the knee joint and the supporting tendons and ligaments and can result in bone chips.

Over at the knee or buck-kneed is not considered as severe as back at the knee because the joint will bend in that direction, but it can still cause added stress to the joint and surrounding structures.

Short, Upright Pasterns/ Long, Sloping Pasterns

Short upright pasterns don't dissipate concussion very well as it moves up the leg. This jarring effect can create soundness problems, including arthritis in the pastern joint and navicular disease (a degenerative condition affecting the navicular bone — small bone in the back of the foot).

Long, sloping pasterns tend to be weaker, and in some cases the fetlock will hit the ground as the horse moves at speed. Some horses may have long pasterns that are more upright, and as with the short upright pasterns, concussion is not dissipated through the leg properly.

Hind End Conformation

A horse's powerfully muscled hind end is the engine, propelling the animal forward as it runs. Stockier sprinter types tend to have more heavily muscled hindquarters than their leaner, rangier counterparts, enabling them to employ quick bursts of speed. The hind legs also act as a horse's brakes, helping the horse check his momentum quickly, such as in traffic in a race. Thus, while the hind legs don't receive the same amount of concussion as the front legs, good conformation is still necessary to keep the horse sound and performing to the best of its ability. As you would with the front legs, to determine the ideal conformation from a side view, start your imaginary line at the rear of the buttocks and drop down to the hock, then along the back of the cannon bone to the ground. The horse's pasterns should angle away from the line in the 50- to 55-degree range. *(See illustration below at left.)* If you are looking at the horse from behind, the imaginary line should run ver-

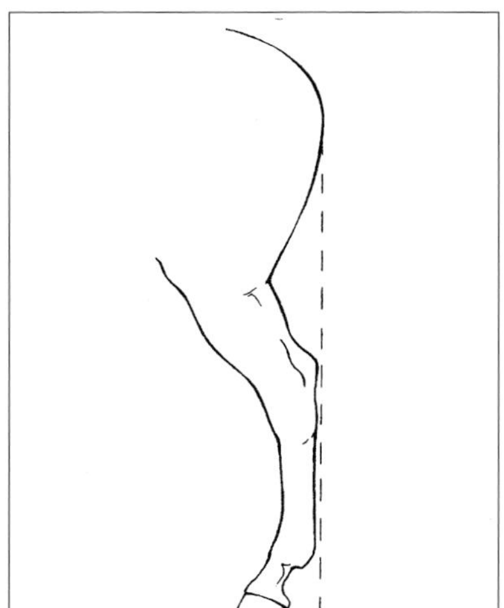

Ideal hind leg conformation

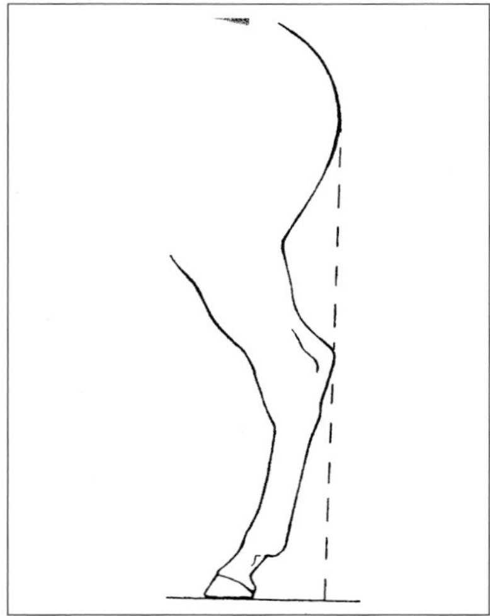

Sickle-hocked

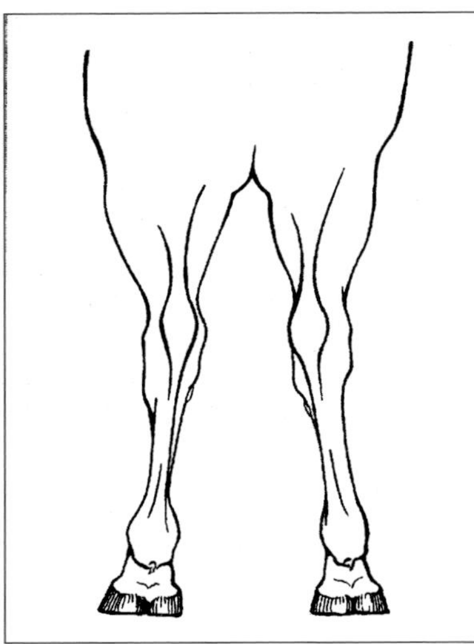

Cow-hocked

tically from the top of the buttocks through the hock down to the ground.

Below are some of the main hind-leg faults you will encounter as you examine horses.

Sickle-hocked

A horse that is sickle-hocked will have cannon bones that are placed forward of that imaginary ideal vertical line. *(See illustration on previous page.)* The hock itself will line up properly. If this fault is severe, the hock can be compromised by the added stress placed on it and could predispose a horse to developing curbs (swellings in a tendon sheath at the base of the hock) or bone spavin (a bony growth at the hock).

Straight Behind

Straight behind means there is not much angle between the thigh bone (femur) and tibia. You can see this fault by looking at the horse in profile. This condition can place added stress on the stifle joint and hock because concussion is not dissipated as effectively through the leg.

Cow-hocked

You can tell a cow-hocked horse by looking at it from behind. The hocks will appear closer together while the feet will be spread apart and often turned out. Depending on the severity of the defect, added stress placed on the hock, especially to the inside, can cause soundness problems. In addition, because the feet are turned out, a horse could strike itself on the opposite leg as it moves.

Base Narrow

A horse that is base narrow has feet that are closer together than the hocks and thighs, giving the animal a bow-legged appearance when viewed from behind. This is a serious fault, especially in a performance animal because the horse won't be able to propel itself forward or brake efficiently, and with the legs being out of alignment, the stresses from the horse's footfalls can quickly add up to injury and soundness issues.

The Feet

Don't forget to examine a horse's hooves. Foot conformation is very important for any horse but especially so for athletes. Feet should be proportionate to the size and weight of the horse with a strong hoof wall (the support structure) and a slightly concave sole (bottom of the foot). Front feet tend to be stronger and rounder than hind feet because of the extra concussion the front end takes. Note hooves that are brittle or cracking; the horse may have naturally weak hooves that are prone to such problems. Or, improper nutrition, bad living conditions (too wet or too dry), or illness could be the cause.

Other Conformation Faults

Some other conformation flaws that many horsemen tend to avoid include a swayed back, a ewe neck, and pig eyes. You can observe these flaws during your overall examination of a horse's body. A horse with a swayed back might be long and weak in the back and develop chronic back soreness or other problems. In addition, in some cases, it might be difficult to fit a saddle properly.

A ewe-necked horse has a neck that comes low out of the shoulder, dipping down in front of the withers. Horses with this flaw tend to be high-headed and can be difficult to train because the neck has less flexion at the poll (point behind the ears where the head joins the neck), giving a rider less control.

A horse that has "pig eyes" has eyes that are small and close set, which could impair the horse's range of vision; this flaw is considered by many horsemen to indicate laziness or stubbornness. Ideally, the horse's eyes should be wide set, alert, and bright.

A flaw that turns off some horsemen but doesn't necessarily affect performance is a buck-toothed or parrot-mouth appearance, in which the horse has a severe underbite, with its lower and upper jaws not meeting properly. Depending on the severity of this flaw, a horse's eating ability, especially grazing, could be impaired.

Breeding Type to Type

Most Thoroughbred breeders follow the old adage of "breed the best to the best and hope for the best." But what is probably more accurate is "breed a relatively sound stallion to a relatively sound mare and hope for a relatively sound offspring."

As stated earlier, conformation

ANNE M. EBERHARDT

Look for a stallion that is well-balanced whether large or small in build

comes down to genetics. *(See Chapter 6 for a further discussion of genetics.)* In breeding type to type, you want to find a stallion that not only is balanced similarly to your mare but also has similar desirable conformation traits that could be transferred to the offspring. It also helps to learn all you can about the previous couple of generations in the stallion's pedigree (grandparents/great-grandparents). Is the sire line known for getting horses with certain faults or good qualities? What about the female family? Remember, when evaluating a horse, you can't go on just conformation; nor can you rely just on pedigree. The two are intertwined and the more you learn about both, the more confident you will be in selecting mares and their mates.

What you want to avoid is breeding a mare with a serious conformation fault — such as back at the knee — to a stallion with the same fault. You're just genetically doubling your chances of getting a foal that is back at the knee. You also shouldn't breed a small mare to a big stallion (or vice versa) in hopes of getting a medium-sized foal — though many breeders adhere to this philosophy. More than likely the foal will be either small or big, because either the "big" gene or "short" gene will be expressed. But if your small mare and the large stallion are both well-balanced individuals for their size (your mare is not too compact and the stallion is not too rangy), then their offspring has a good chance of being well balanced, too, whether large or small in stature.

By Judy L. Marchman

Pedigree Theories

Racehorse breeding theories have existed for as long as horsemen have tried to produce a good horse. Whether art or science, these theories seek to increase the probability of success.

You are already familiar with the concept of the family tree, as in the old adage "that apple didn't fall far from its tree." So when Baby Jacob is said to have his great-granddaddy's cowlick or little Annie has inherited her mother's eyes, some of the physical characteristics inherent in those names on the chart are manifesting themselves. A pedigree is nothing more than a generational representation of a particular horse's family tree, and while the chart may look a little strange to the novice, it is merely a blueprint of that horse's lineage and genetic qualities.

Pedigree charts come in various depths: three-cross (as is commonly found in most sales catalogs), four-cross (as is commonly found in *The Blood-Horse* and most other industry publications), or five-cross (as is commonly found in most pedigree reports from companies that specialize in Thoroughbred data, such as The Jockey Club Information Systems). More crosses are available but they are usually through computer programs such as CompuSire and Tesio Power. Pedigree specialists and bloodstock agents also can provide more in-depth pedigrees. As you look at the chart, the male relatives are always the top portion of the paired names and the female relatives, the bottom. But there's much more to pedigrees than just recognizing and reading the parts of a chart.

Remember that basic biology class in high school or college and how most of us were glad to have it on our transcripts as a passing grade in a course that satisfied some graduation requirement. What a relief to think that this (like those story problems in math about trains leaving Chicago) was something we would never have to deal with again. Well, we were wrong. Just when we thought it was safe, it has come back to haunt us. For the basis of pedigree theories lies in science, more specifically biology and most specifically that branch that deals in the world of DNA helices — genetics. Therefore, as a prelude to examining pedigree theories, it

THINGS TO KNOW

- A pedigree is a horse's family tree.
- The top half of the pedigree denotes the sire and his antecedents while the bottom half shows the same for the dam.
- Pedigree theories evolved in attempts to breed better, faster racehorses.
- Inbreeding, linebreeding, outcrossing, and nicks are among the most common pedigree theories.

might be useful to review some of the most basic principles of genetics. And, yes, there will be a test. It will not come with a blue book but in the unforgiving real world, and you won't know your grade for a year or more.

Genes are pieces of DNA (deoxyribonucleic acid), the genetic material of the cell, that contain information and coding for characteristics both visible (such as hair and eye color, height, etc.) and invisible (such as intelligence, a susceptibility to certain diseases, athleticism, etc.). All animals carry two copies of each gene, one inherited from each parent. If the offspring has inherited two different copies of the same gene, it is said to be heterozygous. If one copy dominates the other, the dominated copy is said to be recessive. If both copies of the gene are the same, the offspring is said to be homozygous. In order for a recessive gene to be expressed, the offspring must be homozygous for that trait. Let's look at an example.

The following pedigree chart of the great Secretariat also provides the coat color for each of his ancestors. Secretariat was the modern-day Big Red, so called because of his gleaming copper chestnut coloring. However, looking at the chart, we find that his sire (Bold Ruler) was dark bay or brown and his dam (Somethingroyal) was bay. The second generation also contains no chestnut horses. On the sire side of the pedigree, the first chestnut appears in the third generation: Bold Ruler's dam is by the chestnut Discovery, a grandson of the chestnut Fair Play (the sire of the original Big Red, the immortal Man o' War). On the female side of the pedigree, the first chestnut appears in the fourth generation with Polymelian. With so many bays in the first four generations, how did Secretariat get to be a chestnut? The gene for chestnut color is recessive; therefore, in order for it to be expressed, Secretariat had to inherit a chestnut gene from his sire and a chestnut gene from his dam. Although we cannot say for certain from which ancestors Secretariat inherited his chestnut genes, we can see from studying the pedigree chart how those genes were carried from generation to generation. This gives us some indication that the more we know about the horses in the past generations, the more we understand about the horse in the present.

Physical characteristics are visible and, therefore, easily recognized, but genes pass more than just physical characteristics. Essentially, those unseen characteristics form the genetic pool that Thoroughbred breeders are trying to tap: speed, stamina, soundness.

Bloodstock breeding is an "inexact" science. It's a giant spin of the genetic roulette wheel. Sometimes you get red when you bet on black and vice versa, but sometimes you hit the exact combination. And those occasions keep you coming back to the table again and again. One horse can be a champion and his full brother a nag. Choosing the perfect stallion to match your mare is a daunting task but one that is accompanied by a great deal of satisfaction, especially when you see the colt or filly from a mating you have planned cross the finish line first and validate your selection.

As formidable as planning a mating might seem, you are not left totally in the dark.

Centuries of breeding have provided several theories as guides to breeding faster and better horses.

But remember: These are theories in every sense of the word. Theories are nothing more than generalizations concerning why or how something is the way it is. Therefore, no pedigree theory should be taken as gospel. Rather, each is merely a tool, albeit a very complex tool. And it falls upon breeders to gain as much knowledge as possible before deciding the method — or combination of methods — with which they feel most comfortable.

Pedigree theories are as diverse as the breeders who use them. The theories range from the non-scientific yet always sage "breed the best to the best and hope for the best" to the pseudo-scientific use of horoscopes and astrology (Lord Wavertree's method. Don't snicker. He bred the following English classic winners: Two Thousand Guineas and Derby winner Minoru, One

Secretariat	Bold Ruler, dark bay	Nasrullah, bay	Nearco, brown	Pharos, bay	Phalaris, brown
					Scapa Flow, ch
				Nogara, bay	Havresac II, dk b
					Catnip, bay
			Mumtaz Begum, bay	Blenheim II, brown	Blandford, brown
					Malva, b
				Mumtaz Mahal, grey	The Tetrarch, gr
					Lady Josephine, ch
		Miss Disco, bay	Discovery, ch	Display, bay	Fair Play, ch
					Cicuta, b
				Ariadne, brown	Light Brigade, br
					Adrienne, ch
			Outdone, bay	Pompey, ch	Sun Briar, b
					Cleopatra, ch
				Sweep Out, bay	Sweep On, b
					Dugout, b
	Somethingroyal, bay	Princequillo, bay	Prince Rose, bay	Rose Prince, bay	Prince Palatine, b
					Eglantine, b
				Indolence, bay	Gay Crusader, b
					Barrier, gr
			Cosquilla, bay	Papyrus, brown	Tracery, br
					Miss Matty, b
				Quick Thought, bay	White Eagle, ch
					Mindful, b
		Imperatrice, dark bay	Caruso, bay	Polymelian, ch	Polymelus, b
					Pasquita, ch
				Sweet Music, bay	Harmonicon, ch
					Isette, dk b
			Cinquepace, bay	Brown Bud, brown	Brown Prince, br
					June Rose, b
				Assignation, brown	Teddy, b
					Cinq a Sept, ch

Secretariat's pedigree

Thousand Guineas and Oaks winner Cherry Lass, One Thousand Guineas winner Witch Elm, and St. Leger winners Prince Palatine and Night Hawk). Somewhere between lies the science, and these theories whose bases lie in science need consideration. This section merely serves as an overview. Each theory could sustain a chapter in itself and invites further exploration. Like beauty in the eye of the beholder, each theory is subjective; therefore, each has its proponents and its detractors.

Inbreeding and Linebreeding

Inbreeding and linebreeding are essentially the same thing. Both involve this basic concept: selectively breeding back to superior ancestors in order to duplicate the influence of certain positive qualities on the foal. The difference boils down to a matter of degree, and you will find various ideas as

	50%	25%	12.5%	6.25%	3.125%
Lost in the Fog	Lost Soldier	Danzig	Northern Dancer	Nearctic	Nearco Lady Angela
				Natalma	**Native Dancer** **Almahmoud**
			Pas de Nom	Admiral's Voyage	Crafty Admiral Olympia Lou
				Petitioner	Petition Steady Aim
		Lady Winborne	Secretariat	**Bold Ruler**	Nasrullah Miss Disco
				Somethingroyal	Princequillo Imperatrice
			Priceless Gem	Hail to Reason	Turn-to Nothirdchance
				Searching	War Admiral Big Hurry
	Cloud Break	Dr. Carter	Caro	Fortino	Grey Sovereign Ranavalo
				Chambord	Chamossaire Life Hill
			Gentle Touch	Chieftain	**Bold Ruler** Pocahontas
				My Dear Girl	Rough'n Tumble Iltis
		Wistful	Maribeau	Ribot	Tenerani Romanella
				Cosmah	Cosmic Bomb **Almahmoud**
			Margaret's Number	Native Charger	**Native Dancer** Greek Blond
				Dungiven	Correlation Jacolee

Lost in the Fog's pedigree showing percentage of each generation's influence

to the line of demarcation that separates the two. Some pedigree experts think that inbreeding occurs only within the first three generations while others stretch it to include four or even five generations. Everything else is linebreeding. Although the point between inbreeding and linebreeding may differ, the principle does not.

For centuries most Thoroughbred breeding has adhered to this principle or has involved a variation of it. Because the modern Thoroughbred traces to just three stallions — Eclipse, Herod, and Matchem — any Thoroughbred is inbred.

Many experts theorize that there is less influence in linebreeding because of the nature of genetics. In the pedigree chart of 2005 sprint champion Lost in the Fog *(opposite)*, each generation has been marked with the amount of influence it has on the entire pedigree. As you move beyond the fifth generation the influence becomes negligible. (By the sixth generation, 1.563 percent; the seventh, .781; the eighth, .391; the ninth, .195) By the time you have reached the tenth generation, there is only .098 percent influence for each ancestor. You can find the influence of each ancestor by multiplying the number of times that ancestor appears in any generation by the percentage for that generation and then add together your calculations.

On the other hand, some pedigree experts feel that the generations farther back are important and attribute to them the role of the engine that drives the rest of the pedigree. For example, a prepotent sire (one that throws offspring similar to himself) is usually a good source of homozygous genes, having been linebred/inbred to the point where he breeds true to the desirable characteristics for which he has been bred.

The purpose of inbreeding/linebreeding is to increase the homozygosity (those genes that are the same) of desirable qualities. Some people also believe that the inbreeding should be achieved by sex-balanced breeding via a son and a daughter of the superior ancestor. Take, for example, the pedigree of American-bred European champion Divine Proportions *(following page)*. (Nureyev [a son of Special] and Sadler's Wells [a grandson of Special through her daughter Fairy Bridge] are three-quarters related.)

However, not all genes are good genes, and the breeder needs to be particularly aware that the result may be homozygosity of undesirable qualities. Inbreeding will not introduce faults but if inbreeding concentrates good qualities, it will also intensify faults already there. (This raises the question of whether we already are seeing the results of inbreeding in the number of bleeders and in the unsoundness of our horses.) For this reason it is important that any breeder know as much about the animals in the pedigree as possible and be as aware of the recessive qualities as of the dominant qualities. If there is a weakness in one horse, don't increase the chances of duplicating that fault in the offspring by breeding to another horse that exhibits the same trait. For example, if you have a mare with offset knees, you probably wouldn't choose a stallion with the same problem because of the likelihood of passing this fault to the offspring. Sometimes, however, what you see is not what you get. Modern veterinary medicine has found a way to correct some of these physical flaws; however, the gene that expresses the problem remains uncorrected and transmittable. For that reason, among others, it is important to know as much about as many horses in the pedigree as possible. So, there's a lot of homework involved.

Outcrossing

On the other side of the inbreeding/linebreeding coin is outcrossing. If a horse is too intensely inbred (too homozygous), it might not be wise to continue with that plan. Rather the idea would be to introduce a little hybrid vigor into the bloodline by choosing a mate devoid or relatively devoid of the dominant blood. The effect of this kind of mating would be to add some new genes to the mix, mov-

Divine Proportions	Kingmambo	Mr. Prospector	Raise a Native	Native Dancer	Polynesian Geisha
				Raise You	Case Ace Lady Glory
			Gold Digger	Nashua	Nasrullah Segula
				Sequence	Count Fleet Miss Dogwood
		Miesque	Nureyev	Northern Dancer	Nearctic Natalma
				Special	Forli Thong
			Pasadoble	Prove Out	Graustark Equal Venture
				Santa Quilla	Sanctus Neriad
	Myth to Reality	Sadler's Wells	Northern Dancer	Nearctic	Nearco Lady Angela
				Natalma	Native Dancer Almahmoud
			Fairy Bridge	Bold Reason	Hail to Reason Lalun
				Special	Forli Thong
		Milliere	Mill Reef	Never Bend	Nasrullah Lalun
				Milan Mill	Princequillo Virginia Water
			Hardiemma	Hardicanute	Hard Ridden Harvest Maid
				Grand Cross	Grandmaster Blue Cross

Divine Proportions' pedigree showing sex-balanced inbreeding

ing the offspring to a more heterozygous animal. For example, Northern Dancer and Mr. Prospector are the dominant sires for inbreeding today. If your mare has too much of this blood, it might be wise to find a mate like Holy Bull, sire of 2005 Kentucky Derby winner Giacomo, who carries none of the Northern Dancer/Mr. Prospector blood in his first five generations.

Many good horses are products of outcrosses: 2005 Horse of the Year Saint Liam, 2004 Horse of the Year Ghostzapper, and 2005 Preakness/Belmont winner Afleet Alex are examples.

Critics point to the fact that the offspring resulting from such a cross, however, might not be able to pass on the quality genes because the gene pool has been diluted by the introduction of the diverse genes from the other side of the pedigree.

Ghostzapper	Awesome Again	Deputy Minister	Vice Regent	Northern Dancer	Nearctic
					Natalma
				Victoria Regina	Menetrier
					Victoriana
			Mint Copy	Bunty's Flight	Bunty Lawless
					Broom Flight
				Shakney	Jabneh
					Grass Shack
		Primal Force	Blushing Groom	Red God	Nasrullah
					Spring Run
				Runaway Bride	Wild Risk
					Aimee
			Prime Prospect	Mr. Prospector	Raise a Native
					Gold Digger
				Square Generation	Olden Times
					Chavalon
	Baby Zip	Relaunch	In Reality	Intentionally	Intent
					My Recipe
				My Dear Girl	Rough'n Tumble
					Iltis
			Foggy Note	The Axe II	Mahmoud
					Blackball
				Silver Song	Royal Note
					Beadah
		Thirty Zip	Tri Jet	Jester	Tom Fool
					Golden Apple
				Haze	Olympia
					Blue Castle
			Sailaway	Hawaii	Utrillo
					Ethane
				Quick Wit	Shannon
					Witty

Ghostzapper's pedigree showing outcrossing

Nicks

One popular theory is based on the affinity of one bloodline for another. This theory is known as a nick. It is based on the belief that there is a successful mingling of blood, a complement of genes that produces a superior individual when certain lines of horses are crossed. One of the most famous of these nicks is the Nasrullah/Princequillo nick. Another is the Bull Lea/Blue Larkspur nick. A contemporary example of a nick would be the Sadler's Wells nick with Darshaan mares. To determine if this is a nick, we must ask the following question: Do Darshaan mares perform better when bred to Sadler's Wells than they do when bred to other stallions?

A good place to start would be to look at the statistics. Our sample will consider the produce of Darshaan mares through 2003, this last crop being three-year-olds

Sadler's Wells	Northern Dancer	Nearctic	Nearco	Pharos	Phalaris
					Scapa Flow
				Nogara	Havresac
					Catnip
			Lady Angela	Hyperion	Gainsborough
					Selene
				Sister Sarah	Abbots Trace
					Sarita
		Natalma	Native Dancer	Polynesian	Unbreakable
					Black Polly
				Geisha	Discovery
					Miyako
			Almahmoud	Mahmoud	Blenheim II
					Mah Mahal
				Arbitrator	Peace Chance
					Mother Goose
	Fairy Bridge	Bold Reason	Hail to Reason	Turn-to	Royal Charger
					Source Sucree
				Nothirdchance	Blue Swords
					Galla Colors
			Lalun	Djeddah	Djebel
					Djezima
				Be Faithful	Bimelech
					Bloodroot
		Special	Forli	Aristophanes	Hyperion
					Commotion
				Trevisa	Advocate
					Veneta
			Thong	Nantallah	Nasrullah
					Shimmer
				Rough Shod II	Gold Bridge
					Dalmary

Sadler's Wells' pedigree

(although many are still unraced and young in their careers). This is a pool of 1,190 named foals. Of those foals, 69 are by Sadler's Wells. A look at the number of stakes winners in relation to the foals will give us an idea as to whether there is an affinity between Darshaan mares and Sadler's Wells. Darshaan mares have produced 86 stakes winners (7 percent). Of those 86 stakes winners, 15 have been by Sadler's Wells (17 percent). What is even more incredible is the quality of those stakes winners: seven of the 15 have won group or grade I stakes (the highest level) and six of those seven have either been named a champion or a high-weight for their divisions. Stallions other than Sadler's Wells have sired 1,121 foals (94 percent), of which 71 are stakes winners (6 percent) while 15 of the 69 foals by Sadler's Wells have won stakes (22 percent).

Darshaan	Shirley Heights	Mill Reef	Never Bend	Nasrullah	Nearco Mumtaz Begum
				Lalun	Djeddah Be Faithful
			Milan Mill	Princequillo	Prince Rose Cosquilla
				Virginia Water	Count Fleet Red Ray
		Hardiemma	Hardicanute	Hard Ridden	Hard Sauce Toute Belle
				Harvest Maid	Umidwar Hay Fell
			Grand Cross	Grandmaster	Atout Maitre Honorarium
				Blue Cross	Blue Peter King's Cross
	Delsey	Abdos	Arbar	Djebel	Tourbillon Loika
				Astronomie	Asterus Likka
			Pretty Lady	Umidwar	Blandford Uganda
				La Moqueuse	Teddy Primrose Lane
		Kelty	Venture	Relic	War Relic Bridal Colors
				Rose o' Lynn	Pherozshah Rocklyn
			Marilla	Marsyas	Trimdon Astronomie
				Albanilla	Pharis Tourzima

Darshaan's pedigree

But nicks also involve patterns, and if we extend our research a bit further, we find that there also seems to be an affinity between Sadler's Wells and Darshaan's sire, Shirley Heights. Shirley Heights mares have produced 146 stakes winners from 1,835 foals (8 percent). Of those stakes winners, 16 have been by Sadler's Wells (11 percent), which leaves other stallions responsible for 130 stakes winners (7 percent) from the number of foals they sired (1,751). The number of Sadler's Wells stakes winners to the number of foals sired by Sadler's Wells from Shirley Heights mares (84) is 19 percent.

In looking at Shirley Heights as well as Darshaan, we were able to see a broader pattern/trend/affinity with Sadler's Wells. Had only Darshaan been examined, it would be possible to miss the broader picture that Sadler's Wells has done well with other representatives of this male line.

The Sadler's Wells/Darshaan Pattern

Darshaan
1,190 named foals from Darshaan mares
86 stakes winners
69 named foals by Sadler's Wells
15 stakes winners by Sadler's Wells

Shirley Heights
1,835 named foals from Shirley Heights mares
146 stakes winners
75 named foals by Sadler's Wells
16 stakes winners by Sadler's Wells

Mill Reef
1,474 named foals from Mill Reef mares
137 stakes winners
40 named foals by Sadler's Wells
8 stakes winners by Sadler's Wells

A next logical step would be to look at Shirley Heights' sire, Mill Reef. How do Mill Reef mares fare when mated to Sadler's Wells? As a broodmare sire, Mill Reef has 139 stakes winners (9 percent) from foals. Mill Reef mares have produced 40 named foals by Sadler's Wells. Of those 40 foals, eight are stakes winners (20 percent) so Mill Reef, like his son and grandson, has daughters that do better when bred to Sadler's Wells than when bred to other sires.

Critics point to several flaws in the nicks theory: that this theory ignores some of the principles of statistical research; that the data are not based on a large enough sample size; and that the variables have not been controlled.

Female Family Inbreeding

This theory seems to be based on the strong opinion held by some that the family is stronger than the individual.

Female family inbreeding occurs when there is a duplication of ancestors using the same female ancestor. Often you will see the term Rasmussen Factor associated with this concept, but there is a limitation. The Rasmussen Factor occurs only when the same female ancestor appears within the first five generations.

What is the science that lies at the root of this theory? Just as the y-chromosome (that which determines if a child is male) can only be inherited from the male, mitochondrial DNA can only be inherited from the female and is passed along from generation to generation (tail female). Mitochondria are the powerhouses of the cell and are responsible for converting energy to fuel the cells in their various functions. Some female families have proven better in this ability to convert energy than others. The doubling or tripling of the blood of these powerhouse mares in a pedigree might have a positive effect on creating superior offspring.

Let's use our Sadler's Wells/Mill Reef line stallions to illustrate. Looking at a five-cross pedigree of Sadler's Wells' grade I winner, In the Wings, we find the mare Lalun 4x5 through the half brothers Bold Reason and Never Bend, respectively (a cross that fits within the five-generation criterion necessary to satisfy the Rasmussen Factor). Descending from the valuable E.R. Bradley family headed by Knockaney Bridge, Lalun won the Kentucky Oaks, Beldame Stakes, and Pageant Stakes and ran second in the Coaching Club American Oaks. As a broodmare, she produced two outstanding classic-placed sons: champion Never Bend

In the Wings	Sadler's Wells	Northern Dancer	Nearctic	Nearco	Pharos
					Nogara
				Lady Angela	Hyperion
					Sister Sarah
			Natalma	Native Dancer	Polynesian
					Geisha
				Almahmoud	Mahmoud
					Arbitrator
		Fairy Bridge	Bold Reason	Hail to Reason	Turn-to
					Nothirdchance
				Lalun	Djeddah
					Be Faithful
			Special	Forli	Aristophanes
					Trevisa
				Thong	Nantallah
					Rough Shod II
	High Hawk	Shirley Heights	Mill Reef	Never Bend	Nasrullah
					Lalun
				Milan Mill	Princequillo
					Virginia Water
			Hardiemma	Hardicanute	Hard Ridden
					Harvest Maid
				Grand Cross	Grandmaster
					Blue Cross
		Sunbittern	Sea Hawk	Herbager	Vandale
					Flagette
				Sea Nymph	Free Man
					Sea Spray
			Pantoufle	Panaslipper	Solar Slipper
					Panastrid
				Etoile de France	Arctic Star
					Miss France

In the Wings' pedigree showing female family inbreeding

and Travers Stakes winner Bold Reason.

Another successful Sadler's Wells cross with the Lalun inbreeding is through Never Bend's son Riverman and Riverman's son Irish River. This cross has produced grade I winners Carnegie, Insight, and Sequoyah.

Though we can't say for certainty that this cross provides the impetus for Sadler's Wells' success, no fewer than 66 of his 267 stakes winners are inbred to Lalun through the sixth generation (24.7 percent) and 21 of his 70 grade I winners carry this inbreeding (30 percent).

Looking at the pedigrees of grade I winners in the United States in 2005, we find that two-year-old champion Stevie Wonderboy is inbred to the outstanding producer Weekend Surprise 3x3 (through the half brothers A.P. Indy and Summer Squall, respectively), and champion older mare Ashado is inbred to the prolific matrons Cosmah 3x5 (through half brothers Halo and Maribeau) and to Almahmoud 4x5 (through half sis-

The following details some of the prominent female family inbreeding found in 2005 stakes winners: Beneath each mare are the descendants that act as the conduits of the blood.

Almahmoud
- Cosmah (filly)
- Natalma (filly)
- Bubbling Beauty (filly)

Cosmah
- Halo (colt)
- Maribeau (colt)
- Queen Sucree (filly)

Natalma
- Northern Dancer (colt)
- Spring Adieu (filly)
- Raise the Standard (filly)

Victoria Regina
- Vice Regent (colt)
- Viceregal (colt)

Weekend Surprise
- A.P. Indy (colt)
- Summer Squall (colt)

Pocahontas
- Tom Rolfe (colt)
- Lady Rebecca (filly)

Trevisa
- Forli (colt)
- Trevisana (filly)

Flower Bowl
- His Majesty (colt)
- Graustark (colt)

Thong
- Special (filly)
- Lisadell (filly)
- Thatch (colt)

Special
- Nureyev (colt)
- Fairy Bridge (filly)

Lalun
- Never Bend (colt)
- Bold Reason (colt)

Somethingroyal
- Secretariat (colt)
- Sir Gaylord (colt)
- Somethingfabulous (colt)

Mixed Marriage
- Tamerett (filly)
- Atan (colt)

Best in Show
- Sex Appeal (filly)
- Monroe (filly)

Sex Appeal
- Try My Best (colt)
- El Gran Senor (colt)

South Ocean
- Storm Bird (colt)
- Oceana (filly)

No Class
- Classy 'n Smart (filly)
- Regal Classic (colt)

Sequence
- Bold Sequence (filly)
- Gold Digger (filly)

Gold Digger
- Mr. Prospector (colt)
- Red Ryder (colt)
- Search for Gold (colt)

My Charmer
- Seattle Slew (colt)
- Lomond (colt)

Glamour
- Poker (colt)
- Intriguing (filly)

Female family inbreeding chart

ters Cosmah and Natalma). Champion sprinter Lost in the Fog is also inbred to Almahmoud (5x5 through Natalma and Cosmah).

Bruce Lowe Family Numbers

Using the Bruce Lowe family numbers is a useful method of keeping track of the various families in a pedigree. However, these numbers, which were at one time integral parts of pedigrees, have lost favor and have disappeared from most published pedigrees. They still may be found on some pedigree Web sites, such as pedigreequery.com.

Bruce Lowe, an Australian pedigree researcher and author of *Breeding Racehorses by the Figure System,* classified the female families by tracing every mare in the English *General Stud Book* to her first known female ancestor to be registered. He then looked at the winners of three of the English

Ashado	Saint Ballado	Halo	Hail to Reason	Turn-to	Royal Charger	9-c
					Source Sucree	1-w
				Nothirdchance	Blue Swords	7
					Galla Colors	4-n
			Cosmah	Cosmic Bomb	Pharamond II	6-e
					Banish Fear	14-f
				Almahmoud	Mahmoud	9-c
					Arbitrato	2-d
		Ballade	Herbager	Vandale	Plassy	13-e
					Vanille	3-c
				Flagette	Escamillo	14-a
					Fidgette	16-c
			Miss Swapsco	Cohoes	Mahmoud	9-c
					Belle of Troy	1-x
				Soaring	Swaps	A4
					Skylarking	12-c
	Goulash	Mari's Book	Northern Dancer	Nearctic	Nearco	4-r
					Lady Angela	14-c
				Natalma	Native Dancer	5-f
					Almahmoud	**2-d**
			Mari Her	Maribeau	Ribot	4-1
					Cosmah	**2-d**
				Hem and Haw	Double Jay	14-a
					Royal Fan	8-a
		Wise Bride	Blushing Groom	Red God	Nasrullah	9-c
					Spring Run	8-c
				Runaway Bride	Wild Risk	3-f
					Aimee	22-d
			Wising Up	Smarten	Cyane	16-b
					Smartaire	A13
				Hardly	Rock Talk	4-n
					Softly	16-g

Ashado's pedigree showing female family inbreeding and Bruce Lowe numbers

Chef-de-race Stallions

Name	*Birth*	*Category*
Abernant	1946	Brilliant
Apalachee	1971	Brilliant
Baldski*	1974	Brilliant
Black Toney*	1911	Brilliant
Blushing Groom*	1974	Brilliant
Bold Ruler*	1954	Brilliant
British Empire	1937	Brilliant
Buckaroo*	1975	Brilliant
Bull Dog	1927	Brilliant
Cicero	1902	Brilliant
Court Martial	1942	Brilliant
Double Jay	1944	Brilliant
Fair Trial	1932	Brilliant
Fairway	1925	Brilliant
Gallant Man*	1954	Brilliant
Grey Dawn II*	1962	Brilliant
Grey Sovereign	1948	Brilliant
Habitat	1966	Brilliant
Halo*	1969	Brilliant
Heliopolis	1936	Brilliant
Hoist the Flag*	1968	Brilliant
Hyperion*	1930	Brilliant
Icecapade*	1969	Brilliant
In Reality*	1964	Brilliant
Intentionally*	1956	Brilliant
Key to the Mint*	1969	Brilliant
King's Bishop*	1969	Brilliant
Mr. Prospector*	1970	Brilliant
My Babu	1945	Brilliant
Nasrullah	1940	Brilliant
Nearco*	1935	Brilliant
Never Bend*	1960	Brilliant
Noholme II*	1956	Brilliant
Northern Dancer*	1961	Brilliant
Olympia	1946	Brilliant
Orby	1904	Brilliant
Panorama	1936	Brilliant
Peter Pan	1904	Brilliant
Phalaris	1913	Brilliant
Pharis II	1936	Brilliant
Pompey	1923	Brilliant
Raise a Native	1961	Brilliant
Reviewer*	1966	Brilliant
Roman	1937	Brilliant
Rough'n Tumble*	1948	Brilliant
Royal Charger	1942	Brilliant
Seattle Slew*	1974	Brilliant
Sharpen Up*	1969	Brilliant
Sir Cosmo	1926	Brilliant
Speak John*	1958	Brilliant
Spy Song	1943	Brilliant
Tudor Minstrel	1944	Brilliant
Turn-to*	1951	Brilliant
Ultimus	1906	Brilliant
What a Pleasure	1965	Brilliant
Ack Ack*	1966	Intermediate
Baldski*	1974	Intermediate
Ben Brush	1893	Intermediate
Big Game	1939	Intermediate
Black Toney*	1911	Intermediate
Bold Bidder*	1962	Intermediate
Bold Ruler*	1954	Intermediate
Broad Brush*	1983	Intermediate
Broomstick	1901	Intermediate
Buckaroo*	1975	Intermediate
Caro*	1967	Intermediate
Chief's Crown*	1982	Intermediate
Colorado	1923	Intermediate
Congreve	1924	Intermediate
Damascus*	1964	Intermediate
Danzig*	1977	Intermediate
Djebel	1937	Intermediate
Dr. Fager	1964	Intermediate
Eight Thirty	1936	Intermediate
Equipoise*	1928	Intermediate
Fappiano*	1977	Intermediate
Full Sail	1934	Intermediate
Gallant Man*	1954	Intermediate
Grey Dawn II*	1962	Intermediate
Havresac II	1915	Intermediate
Hoist the Flag*	1968	Intermediate
Indian Ridge	1985	Intermediate
Intentionally*	1956	Intermediate
Khaled	1943	Intermediate
King Salmon	1930	Intermediate
King's Bishop*	1969	Intermediate
Mahmoud*	1933	Intermediate
Nashua*	1952	Intermediate
Native Dancer*	1950	Intermediate
Never Bend*	1960	Intermediate
Petition	1944	Intermediate
Pharos	1920	Intermediate
Pleasant Colony	1978	Intermediate
Polynesian	1942	Intermediate
Princequillo*	1940	Intermediate
Riverman*	1969	Intermediate
Roman*	1937	Intermediate
Secretariat*	1970	Intermediate
Sir Gaylord*	1959	Intermediate
Sir Ivor*	1965	Intermediate
Speak John*	1958	Intermediate

* — Horse is in more than one category.

Name	Birth	Category
Star Kingdom*	1946	Intermediate
Star Shoot	1898	Intermediate
Sweep	1907	Intermediate
T.V. Lark	1957	Intermediate
The Tetrarch	1911	Intermediate
Tom Fool*	1949	Intermediate
Traghetto	1942	Intermediate
Turn-to*	1951	Intermediate
Ack Ack*	1966	Classic
Alibhai	1938	Classic
Alydar	1975	Classic
Aureole	1950	Classic
Bahram	1932	Classic
Best Turn	1966	Classic
Blandford	1919	Classic
Blenheim II*	1927	Classic
Blue Larkspur	1926	Classic
Blushing Groom*	1974	Classic
Bold Bidder*	1962	Classic
Brantome	1931	Classic
Broad Brush*	1983	Classic
Buckpasser	1963	Classic
Bull Lea	1935	Classic
Caro*	1967	Classic
Clarissimus	1913	Classic
Count Fleet	1940	Classic
Crème dela Crème*	1963	Classic
Damascus*	1964	Classic
Danzig*	1977	Classic
Equipoise*	1928	Classic
Exclusive Native	1965	Classic
Fappiano*	1977	Classic
Forli	1963	Classic
Gainsborough	1915	Classic
Graustark*	1963	Classic
Gundomar	1942	Classic
Hail to Reason	1958	Classic
Halo*	1969	Classic
Herbager*	1956	Classic
High Top	1969	Classic
His Majesty	1968	Classic
Hyperion*	1930	Classic
Icecapade*	1969	Classic
In Reality*	1964	Classic
In the Wings*	1986	Classic
Key to the Mint*	1969	Classic
Luthier	1965	Classic
Lyphard	1969	Classic
Mahmoud*	1933	Classic
Midstream	1933	Classic

Name	Birth	Category
Mill Reef*	1968	Classic
Mossborough	1947	Classic
Mr. Prospector*	1970	Classic
Nashua*	1952	Classic
Native Dancer*	1950	Classic
Navarro	1931	Classic
Nearco*	1935	Classic
Never Say Die	1951	Classic
Nijinsky II*	1967	Classic
Niniski*	1976	Classic
Noholme II*	1956	Classic
Northern Dancer*	1961	Classic
Nureyev	1977	Classic
Persian Gulf	1940	Classic
Pilate	1928	Classic
Pretense	1963	Classic
Prince Bio	1941	Classic
Prince Chevalier	1943	Classic
Prince John	1953	Classic
Prince Rose	1928	Classic
Promised Land	1954	Classic
Reviewer*	1966	Classic
Ribot*	1952	Classic
Riverman*	1969	Classic
Roberto	1969	Classic
Rock Sand*	1900	Classic
Rougn'n Tumble*	1948	Classic
Sadler's Wells*	1981	Classic
Seattle Slew*	1974	Classic
Secretariat*	1970	Classic
Sharpen Up*	1969	Classic
Shirley Heights*	1975	Classic
Sicambre	1948	Classic
Sideral	1948	Classic
Sir Gallahad III	1920	Classic
Sir Gaylord	1959	Classic
Sir Ivor*	1965	Classic
Star Kingdom*	1946	Classic
Swynford	1907	Classic
Ticino*	1939	Classic
Tom Fool*	1949	Classic
Tom Rolfe*	1962	Classic
Tourbillon*	1928	Classic
Tracery	1909	Classic
Vaguely Noble*	1965	Classic
Vieux Manoir	1947	Classic
War Admiral	1934	Classic
Asterus	1923	Solid
Bachelor's Double	1906	Solid
Ballymoss	1954	Solid

Chef-de-race Stallions (Continued)

Name	*Birth*	*Category*
Blenheim II*	1927	Solid
Bois Roussel	1935	Solid
Busted	1963	Solid
Chaucer	1900	Solid
Chief's Crown*	1982	Solid
Crème dela Crème*	1963	Solid
Discovery	1931	Solid
Fair Play*	1905	Solid
Graustark*	1963	Solid
Herbager*	1956	Solid
In the Wings*	1986	Solid
Man o' War	1917	Solid
Mill Reef*	1968	Solid
Nijinsky II*	1967	Solid
Oleander	1924	Solid
Pia Star	1961	Solid
Princequillo*	1940	Solid
Reliance II*	1952	Solid
Relko	1962	Solid
Right Royal	1958	Solid
Rock Sand*	1900	Solid
Round Table	1954	Solid
Sadler's Wells*	1981	Solid
Sea-Bird	1962	Solid
Stage Door Johnny*	1965	Solid
Sunstar	1908	Solid
Tantieme	1947	Solid
Teddy	1913	Solid
Ticino*	1939	Solid
Vatout	1926	Solid
Worden	1949	Solid
Admiral Drake	1931	Professional
Alacantara II	1908	Professional
Alizier	1947	Professional
Alycidon	1945	Professional
Bayardo	1906	Professional
Bruleur	1910	Professional
Chateau Bouscaut	1927	Professional
Crepello	1954	Professional
Dark Ronald	1905	Professional
Donatello II	1934	Professional
Ela-Mana-Mou	1976	Professional
Fair Play*	1905	Professional
Foxbridge	1930	Professional
Hurry On	1913	Professional
La Farina	1911	Professional
Le Fabuleux	1961	Professional
Massine	1920	Professional
Mieuxce	1933	Professional
Niniski	1976	Professional
Ortello	1926	Professional
Precipitation	1933	Professional
Rabelais	1900	Professional
Reliance II	1962	Professional
Ribot	1952	Professional
Run the Gantlet	1968	Professional
Sardanapale	1911	Professional
Shirley Heights*	1975	Professional
Solario	1922	Professional
Son-in-Law	1911	Professional
Spearmint	1903	Professional
Stage Door Johnny*	1965	Professional
Sunny Boy	1944	Professional
Tom Rolfe*	1962	Professional
Tourbillon*	1928	Professional
Vaguely Noble*	1965	Professional
Vandale	1943	Professional
Vatellor	1933	Professional
Wild Risk	1940	Professional

classics (the Derby, Oaks, and St. Leger) and traced their tail-female line of descent. He assigned the family with the most winners of these races as Number 1 Family; the family with the second-most number of winners, Number 2 Family, etc. Originally, there were 43 families. Over time these families were expanded to include American families as well as families from other countries, such as those native to Australia and Argentina. Also, as the families extended through the centuries, sub families were identified within each family. These are designated through the use of a letter attached to the number. For example, 1-x is the designation for the powerful branch headed by La Troienne; 14-c traces back to the great racemare Pretty Polly; 13-c is the branch headed by Stray Shot, and containing the wonderful producer Frizette, tail-female ancestress of Seattle Slew and Mr. Prospector. The fact that sometimes these families go back too far to find the mare that stands at the head of one of the sub-families (sometimes as far back as the nineteenth century) might put off some who question the relevance of a mare in the nineteenth century standing at the head of line today. But as you study more and more of these pedigrees, you will be able to find more contemporary mares that have established their own line for today.

Modern science through mitochondrial DNA testing has found errors in the original Lowe classifications. According to researchers, this new information will affect the pedigrees of every Thoroughbred now living.

Still, the Lowe numbers enable a person studying pedigrees to identify related lines of horses within a larger pedigree and to do it quickly. The more you study the pedigrees with the family numbers, the easier identifying superior branches of these families will be. For example, Family 9-c, tracing back to Americus Girl, is the family of the great sires Nasrullah, Mahmoud, Royal Charger, Fair Trial, and Tudor Minstrel; Family 16-a belongs to the great producer Plucky Liege, responsible for Sir Gallahad III, Bull Dog, Bois Roussel, and Admiral Drake. Knowing more of the details of the members of the individuals in the Bruce Lowe families might help you understand more of how you can use the pedigree to your advantage.

Chef-de-race Sires and Dosage

Dosage is a mathematical computation based on pedigree that Thoroughbred breeders use to classify a horse's ability to run certain distances. The idea is that some sires transmit speed to their offspring while others transmit stamina; therefore, the index is based on only the sires in the first four generations of a horse's pedigree.

From the early part of the twentieth century, influential sires have been identified and divided into five categories or aptitudinal groups: Brilliant (B), Intermediate (I), Classic (C), Solid (S), and Professional (P). These categories cover the spectrum. At one end lies Brilliant, which denotes horses with raw speed and that are best at short distances. At the opposite end lies Professional, which denotes horses that have stamina and are able to sire offspring that can go long distances.

Lt. Col. J.J. Vullier, a French pedigree researcher, developed the idea by observing that certain stallions appeared quite frequently in the pedigrees of the best runners. Thus was born the idea of the "chef-de-race" stallions. Dr. Franco Varola, an Italian breeding expert, carried on his work but added the idea of the aptitudinal traits that these chef-de-race stallions passed on to their progeny. These traits often differed from what the stallions exhibited as runners. For example, as a runner a horse might not have won beyond six furlongs but as a stallion, he might have sired horses that were better at distances beyond a mile. Dr. Steven A. Roman has carried the concept into modern times.

After a horse has been identified as a chef-de-race, he is placed into one or two of the five aptitudinal groups. For example, the great sire Northern Dancer is listed as both Brilliant and Classic while the great Buckpasser falls in the Classic category only. *(See list of chef-de-race stallions in this chapter.)*

Points (based on the generation in which the stallion appears) are then assigned to each time one of these stallions appears in the pedigree. A mathematical formula is used to determine the offspring's Dosage Index (DI). The higher the number of the DI, the more speed-oriented the horse is; the lower the number, the more stamina-oriented. For more information on how the formula works, visit www.chef-de-race.com.

Some pedigree Web sites will let you plan a hypothetical mating. Some of these sites will even figure the DI for you. For example, if you have a mare that you think needs some speed bred into her foals, you can test which stallions you are considering as mates have the best possibility of injecting the necessary speed into the foal. Most of these sites charge a fee for this service.

Dosage critics point to the fact that if a stallion is not a chef-de-race, his influence is omitted and the female sides of the families are not taken into consideration.

In the art and science of breeding, pedigree is just one component. A horse's ancestors provide valuable clues to its potential and its value but other important elements come into play, such as conformation and temperament. What works on paper may not work when the physical characteristics of the mare and stallion are taken into account. You might devise a brilliant breeding on paper with all the right nicks and crosses, but if you don't consider how the parents match up physically, the resulting foal may be a conformational nightmare with a temper to match.

It is worth reiterating: Any of these theories are merely theories and that they are nothing more than tools to help you plan the best mating you can with the money you have to achieve the best possibility for success.

Do your homework. Study the great breeders from both past and present. Ponder their methods. Pore over as many pedigrees as you can. Look at the total progeny of a stallion; see if you can find patterns in the pedigrees of his most successful offspring. Once you've done that, look at his sire and grandsire. It's a lot of work, but the more diligent you are in studying, the more all of the pieces of this complicated puzzle will fall into place and the glass through which you are looking will not seem as dark.

By Tom Hall

Mating Theories: Success Stories

Like solving a jigsaw puzzle, the art of breeding Thoroughbreds requires finding the pieces that fit together. Each breeder does this in his or her own way, and though the similarities are many, the subtleties are legion.

For many breeders, practical considerations determine most of their mating decisions. For instance, they want to send their mares to stallions of a particular stud fee range, or they wish to breed to horses in a particular region of the country.

For other breeders, more theoretical considerations are paramount. Breeding theories and advisers who are specialists in the theories of mating often help breeders determine the most likely crosses to produce good racehorses.

Both theoretical and practical considerations come together as an art or craft in the production of the very best horses that win classic races and become stallions at elite breeding farms.

Practical Selection and the Breeding of Seattle Slew

Seth Hancock, as president of legendary Claiborne Farm for more than three decades, has been responsible for matings that have produced such horses as leading sire Nureyev, champion and multiple classic winner Swale, champion and leading sire Forty Niner, multiple Breeders' Cup Mile winner Lure, the promising young sire Pulpit, and a host of graded stakes winners.

With results like these, clearly Hancock knows his business and weighs many factors as he plans matings for Claiborne's mares, as well as for those of some of the farm's clients.

"If I mate fifty mares, maybe only eight or ten would jump off the page at you, showing a reason for that mating," Hancock said, adding that the rest are bred for practical reasons, as they are at most farms.

For one thing, farm owners are hemmed in by economics because almost every sizable Thoroughbred farm is to some extent a commercial operation. An owner cannot, for instance, breed a stakes-winning mare to a $1,000 stallion and expect any significant profit at the sales, no matter how impressive the planning or pedigree.

Nor can a breeder send a stakes winner or other good mare to even a $10,000 stallion with much confidence of a reasonable return. Instead, valuable mares have to go to valuable stallions, and at

Claiborne, Hancock grades the mares and stallions, sending the best mares to the best stallions.

"We grade Claiborne mares (and stallions) one, two, three for racing class and pedigree," he said. "And I try to breed the mares that are ones to stallions that are ones, and so forth. You can't be economically foolish about things."

Hancock offered a hypothetical example of the way that much of the selection process is dictated by practical considerations. In selecting mares to go to a superior stallion like Triple Crown winner Seattle Slew, Hancock noted, "Claiborne might have, say, 50 mares and only 12 would deserve consideration to go to Seattle Slew. So right off the bat, you throw out 38 of the mares just on the grade" for quality or performance.

"Seattle Slew was an exceptional racehorse and stood for a lot of money," Hancock said. "As a result, not very many mares really had the merit to go to him. That's one of the ways that economics will make a lot of decisions for you."

When the farm actually did arrange to breed mares to Seattle Slew in his first two years at stud, in 1979 and 1980, Claiborne did so in a foal-sharing arrangement with Equusequity Stable, the stable name of the two couples who had raced the Triple Crown champion.

Equusequity had its pick of the resulting colts, including subsequent champion Slew o' Gold from the first crop; the second year produced champion Swale, who won the Derby and Belmont in the Claiborne colors.

As part of the process of matching mares with stallions, Hancock sends mares to selected stallions after also considering size and conformation, nature of the horses, and grade or class of the horses, and then makes decisions regarding pedigree.

He noted that "many decisions in making up a mating are so natural that I wouldn't take any credit for following what has already been proven. Obviously, if you're breeding Mr. Prospector mares to A.P. Indy, for instance, everyone would know to do that."

One of the reasons that breeders know to follow this successful pattern is that A.P. Indy, a champion son of Seattle Slew, sired some major winners out of Mr. Prospector mares from his very first crop to race. These included Tomisue's Delight, Accelerator, and Pulpit. The latter is a Claiborne homebred who, to date, also has become his sire's most accomplished son at stud.

Mating A.P. Indy to Mr. Prospector mares became a popular cross because it worked immediately to produce several really good racehorses. A.P. Indy's sire, Seattle Slew, and paternal grandsire, Bold Reasoning, also became immediate successes at stud with their early runners. Seattle Slew, for instance, was among the first crop of foals by his sire.

And Hancock had a role in the making of Seattle Slew.

"I remember the mating that produced Seattle Slew pretty well," Hancock said, "although it's been more than 30 years. Mr. (Ben) Castleman was awful nice to credit me for helping to breed him, but the plan was really simple.

"When My Charmer came off the track, she was a stakes winner and had a nice pedigree tracing back to Myrtlewood. [A daughter of the stallion Blue Larkspur, Myrtlewood was champion sprinter of 1936 and such an outstanding producer of racehorses that she was instrumental in making Spendthrift Farm a leading breeder. She is the fifth-generation dam in the direct female line of Seattle Slew.] My Charmer might not have been a one [on the Claiborne grading system] at that time, but she was a two, and Bold Reasoning, who was a $5,000 stallion, was only a three."

Bold Reasoning did not rate more highly when he went to stud because his race record and pedigree were good but not extraordinary. As a racehorse, Bold Reasoning had won eight of 12 starts while showing excellent speed, but his most important victory came in the Jersey Derby, not in the classics or in the championship races against older horses.

He didn't even win a stakes at four, which also cost him some prestige among the sales-savvy Kentucky breeders.

But even though he began his stud career for a moderate fee, "Bold Reasoning was the real deal," Hancock said. "He would have been a monster stallion for us if he had lived."

Bold Reasoning died early in his third season at stud and sired only 67 foals. Of those, 10 were stakes winners and 21 others were stakes-placed. The best of his progeny were Seattle Slew and Super Concorde, a colt from Bold Reasoning's second crop who was the highweight two-year-old colt in France in 1977, the year that Seattle Slew won the Triple Crown.

In My Charmer, Hancock said, Castleman "had a nice mare coming off the track, and he was looking for a young sire within his budget. All I said was that 'we've got a nice horse here in Bold Reasoning, he's pretty good look-

ANNE M. EBERHARDT

Seattle Slew

LOUISE E. REINAGEL

Saint Ballado

ing, had a lot of speed,' and that is where he wanted to be price wise. He was nice enough to breed the mare to Bold Reasoning, and the rest is history."

If only all history were so straightforward. Other successful matings are the result of months, even years, of study into the depths of pedigrees.

'Les' is More: Deep research led to champion

Pedigree adviser and matings consultant Les Brinsfield, for instance, has devoted decades to studying the intricacies of pedigrees and the patterns that produce fast racehorses.

While the goal for all pedigree researchers and advisers is to produce good horses, the mating strategies they employ differ. Some prefer nicks (the crossing of particular lines that have bred successful winners before such as the nick of A.P. Indy and Mr. Prospector), and others prefer inbreeding or linebreeding (mating horses that have ancestors in common), while some prefer the arcane approach of dosage (trying to estimate with statistics whether horses will have more stamina or speed).

One of Brinsfield's primary approaches is linebreeding: "That means doubling the strains you've already got. You are looking for the best strains in the pedigree that are strong and seemingly dominant," he said.

Selecting the pedigree elements that are strongest and most dominant is a subtle process. But Brinsfield has spent many hours researching these elements and prefers to build up concentrations of ancestors deep in the pedigrees of horses that he mates.

The location of the common ancestors within the pedigree distinguishes inbreeding from linebreeding.

Brinsfield said, "The difference

between linebreeding and inbreeding is kind of like the distinction between when an egg becomes a chicken. Some people say that any duplicated ancestors closer than the fourth generation is inbreeding, and anything farther back is linebreeding. In either approach, you are doubling up on a common strain, whether you're mating horses with common ancestors 3x3 or 7x7."

(The notation of 3x3 is read as "three by three" and indicates that the duplicated ancestors are both in the third generation of the pedigree. Duplications need not be from the same generation, such as Bold Ruler 4x5x7, which is read as "four by five by seven to Bold Ruler," indicating Bold Ruler in each of those generations.)

As a matings analyst, Brinsfield prefers to use linebreeding when called on to offer his opinions about matings.

For instance, 2005's leading stallion in North America, Saint Ballado, stood at the Taylor family's Taylor Made Farm, a vast boarding, breeding, and sales operation near Lexington, Kentucky.

Several years ago, in an effort to help make Saint Ballado as successful a stallion as possible, the Taylors contacted Brinsfield about finding the most compatible mates for the stallion in terms of pedigree.

In most cases, breeders come to pedigree advisers with a mare or several mares and ask the adviser to find stallions to suit the mares.

In this case, the Taylors started with the stallion and used Brinsfield's suggestions to help select the book.

One of the mares Brinsfield picked out as having special potential for Saint Ballado was the Mari's Book mare Goulash, who showed enough racing ability to win stakes. Duncan Taylor, president of Taylor Made, said that "due to the potential that Les saw in her, we actually bought Goulash for Mr. [Aaron] Jones [a significant shareholder in the stallion] specifically to breed to Saint Ballado."

From four matings with Saint Ballado, Goulash has produced three stakes horses, including Ballado's Halo, who ran third in a pair of stakes, and Saint Stephen, who was third in the National Museum of Racing Hall of Fame Handicap at Saratoga. The third offspring was the homerun: Ashado.

A major stakes winner at two, three, and four, Ashado was champion of her division at three and four. Her most prestigious victories include the Kentucky Oaks and Breeders' Cup Distaff, and after her retirement in the fall of 2005, she sold for $9 million as a broodmare prospect at the Keeneland November breeding stock sale.

The fourth offspring from the mating plan is Sunriver, a three-year-old colt of 2006 (he finished third in the Florida Derby, a major Kentucky Derby prep race).

In explaining the ideas that helped create the profile for suitable matches that he developed for Saint Ballado, Brinsfield noted, "One of my approaches is to linebreed the stallion to the strongest strains in his family. One thing that I look for is the opportunity to breed a stallion back to mares from his own family, and since Saint Ballado had one of the strongest female influences in Almahmoud already in his pedigree, I wanted to be able to double or triple up on

BARBARA D. LIVINGSTON

Monarchos winning the Kentucky Derby

Almahmoud."

Almahmoud is an important taproot broodmare and is the direct female-line ancestor of the leading stallions Northern Dancer and Halo. (Being a taproot mare means that a broodmare was not only a grand producer but that her daughters and sons also produced more racehorses that won or placed in stakes.)

Almahmoud's daughter Natalma produced Northern Dancer as her first foal. The small bay won the 1964 Kentucky Derby and Preakness, then became the most important and successful international stallion of the 1970s and '80s.

One of Almahmoud's other daughters, Cosmah, produced Halo among her many fine offspring. Halo sired Kentucky Derby winner Sunny's Halo, as well as Horse of the Year Sunday Silence, who won the Kentucky Derby, Preakness, and Breeders' Cup Classic. Halo's other offspring include the champions Devil's Bag and Glorious Song, as well as their stakes-winning full brother, Saint Ballado.

The most common avenue for inbreeding or linebreeding to Almahmoud is through Northern Dancer and Halo.

In his linebreeding approach, Brinsfield was hoping not only to duplicate Almahmoud in Saint Ballado's mates but, if possible, to add a third cross of the mare to the matings for Saint Ballado.

Brinsfield said, "In sending Goulash to Saint Ballado, not only do you triple Almahmoud, but there's no doubling of Northern Dancer and Halo." Without inbreeding to Northern Dancer or Halo, the only pedigree influence that is repeated is the mare herself.

The Classics: the art of pedigrees and racehorses

The focus of most high-end breeding programs is the development of classic-caliber racing stock. These are the horses that race in the Kentucky Derby, Preakness, and Belmont as three-year-olds and that command both the greatest respect and economic return.

One breeder who has tasted the wine of classic success is Jim Squires. He bred 2001 Kentucky Derby winner Monarchos from his small band of broodmares at Two Bucks Farm, which Squires operates with his wife, Mary Anne.

After starting in the world of Quarter Horse and Paint Horse breeding, Squires successfully ventured into Thoroughbreds. He espouses an approach that emphasizes the broodmare's influence, while considering other factors, as well.

He said, "One lesson I brought from the Quarter Horse world is that the mare is 80 to 85 percent of the equation. A top mare is the keystone to producing a good foal, and there are some awfully good mares who are not black-type producers."

The emphasis on selecting the right mare has given Squires a recipe for the type of broodmare he prefers. He said, "I like a mare with elegance and femininity; all the mares I have are pretty, and none could be mistaken for a gelding. In addition, I want them to have short cannons, good size and bone, plus a lot of power. And to get them on my budget, I buy mares that people have failed with and hope that I can do something with them that somebody else couldn't."

Trying to select a diamond in the rough is a game undertaking but one that Squires finds a fascinating part of breeding. In purchasing Regal Band, the dam of Monarchos, Squires found a mare with the qualities he was looking for.

Physically, she was a coveted type of mare, feminine but with muscularity and depth through the body. She had good balance and length and was not so strongly made that she appeared masculine.

She was also a mare who had not done well for her owner.

By the excellent broodmare sire Dixieland Band, Regal Band descends from an important Darby Dan Farm foundation family. Regal Band's dam, Regal Roberta, was by Darby Dan's English Derby winner Roberto and was a half sister to three stakes horses, including Rampart Road (by Dixieland Band). The third dam had produced three stakes winners for Darby Dan, and the fourth dam had done the same. This family had formed a key part of the success of Darby Dan Farm through its heyday.

But Regal Band had proven a disappointment for Darby Dan. Her first foal had died, her second was a poor specimen by Meadowlake, and then a third was aborted.

After purchasing the mare from Darby Dan, Squires first bred Regal Band to Secret Hello, a handsome and talented racehorse; then to Black Tie Affair, a late-maturing horse who became Horse of the Year after winning the Breeders' Cup Classic; and then to Maria's Mon, a champion colt at two who had the pedigree of a classic horse, with stamina and speed.

Monarchos was the result of the mating to Maria's Mon.

"He (Monarchos) was such a nice, quality yearling that [bloodstock agent] Murray Smith saw him in my field as a yearling and bought him privately," said Squires.

For Smith, Monarchos sold as a two-year-old in training for $170,000. Then for owner John

Oxley, the gray colt won the Kentucky Derby and Florida Derby at three and became a promising young stallion at Claiborne Farm with his first crop of runners, three-year-olds of 2006.

Regal Band's two preceding foals for Squires also proved quite useful. The colt by Secret Hello was named Morava and became a stakes horse who earned more than $100,000. The Black Tie Affair, a gelding named Resurgence, was still racing in 2006 with earnings of more than $200,000.

Although convinced of the significance of the broodmare in making matings, Squires said, "Another angle of the art of breeding is the prepotency of certain stallions and mares. In many instances, it seems to work like the color gene for dominance. And there seem to be some stallions and mares who are so prepotent you cannot expect to blend with them."

While in most cases, "Regal Band reproduces the stallion" in terms of size, color, and many other traits, Squires said that "in producing Monarchos, it appeared I had bred a blend. He had the strength and quality of Regal Band with some of the length and leg of Maria's Mon. As a racehorse, he appeared more of a blend of his parents, but now that he's been at stud, he's very much like his sire."

ANNE M. EBERHARDT

Claiborne Farm's Seth Hancock

Subtle Differences

While Monarchos was the result of a mating that reproduced many of his sire's best qualities, other matings are the result of different needs.

Hancock noted that "with Lure, it was more of a physical mating. His sire Danzig and dam were different types of horses, and I hoped they would produce a happy medium. Endear was a big, strapping Alydar mare, and Danzig wasn't a real tall horse. It was a physical thing because I thought he could use a little more height and length."

The result of the mating was Lure, a tremendous racehorse with balance and speed. Lure had more leg, combined with the typical Danzig quickness and power, which allowed him to win consecutive runnings of the Breeders' Cup Mile and eight other graded races, while earning more than $2.5 million.

Successful as the combination of different physical traits proved to be with Lure, Hancock varies his approach to fit the horses in question.

"In producing Swale, sending Tuerta to Seattle Slew was more a type-to-type mating," he said. "Seattle Slew was a big horse and a tremendous racehorse and champion. Tuerta was medium-sized and well-balanced, athletic."

The pairing of two horses cast from a similar mold produced dual classic winner Swale, a handsome, near-black colt who won a pair of grade I stakes at two and a trio of grade I races at three.

The seemingly small distinctions behind the matings that produced two such outstanding horses as Lure and Swale illustrate the many decisions that breeders have to make.

Among those choices is whether to emphasize pedigree or physique. Squires said, "I could never breed horses looking at two pieces of paper. I like to look at both parents and also like to see the offspring just to see if they are throwing something from the pedigree behind themselves."

But at the same time that Squires refuses to mate wholly on the basis of pedigree, it still remains a part of his approach. He said, "In researching pedigrees and making the cross on paper, I try not to worry too much about the sire lines, except that I do watch for ways to outcross. When I have an option to inbreed to a wonderful female family, I will hunt for ways to do that."

Other accomplished breeders and their advisers place even greater importance on the pedigree. They want to duplicate the lines in a pedigree in the hope of getting more impact from a significant ancestor by concentrating the potential to express physical qualities or other traits.

Hancock used inbreeding to the great racehorse and sire Round Table as part of his planning that resulted in the graded stakes winner Wend, by Pulpit.

Her dam is the stakes-winning Topsider mare Thread, who is inbred to Round Table 3x3.

"With Pulpit, you bring in Monarchy as the fourth dam," said Hancock. "So that brings in a lot of Knight's Daughter, who was the dam of Monarchy and Round Table, and that's a mating that we saw could bring a lot to the table."

The first foal from this match was the winner Robe, who "was a pretty talented horse," Hancock said, "although he went wrong behind, but it kept us thinking that was the way to go with her (Thread). We've really hammered that cross, and it paid off. The result was Wend and gave us a pretty good mare."

From that result, one might expect Claiborne would try more inbreeding to Round Table with Pulpit, "but we don't have much Round Table left in our broodmare band," Hancock said. "Even though he stood here, he was here a long time ago, and most of those lines are gone. I think the cross has some merit.

"When you're matching stallions and mares, you always consider the physiques of the horses. With Pulpit, he's a medium-sized horse, and I don't think you need to worry too much about size in matching him with mares. He's well-balanced, plenty of bone, but needs some attention to soundness. There wasn't a sounder horse than Round Table, and inbreeding to him satisfies the consideration for soundness."

The use of duplicate lines of the same ancestor, called inbreeding or linebreeding, is typically used to bring more of that ancestor's dominant traits into play with its descendants.

Brinsfield encourages linebreeding because it "means doubling the strains you've already got. You are looking for the best strains that are strong and seemingly dominant. The animal you have is the blueprint you're working on, and when you're working with a mare who doesn't have the prevalent strains in the breed at the time, then you're in trouble unless you're lucky enough to find a stallion with the same rare strains. And it's not just any kind of doubling. It has to be a positive attribute that you're doubling: soundness, speed, courage, or something like that."

Brinsfield recognizes that some breeders are opposed to duplicating strains, even farther back in pedigrees where he prefers to work with the delicate dominance of remote ancestors. He isn't offended at differing approaches but said, "I have a theory that if you are doing something for a principled reason, whether you're right or wrong, you are about 10 times more likely to have some success rather than if you're just throwing balls up in the air."

Breeding good horses is a fascinating game with room for plenty of opinions. Breeding the racehorse is a combination of art, horsemanship, and science. It offers great rewards and excitement and provides pleasures and frustrations, like any other endeavor with animals. After working to "get the mating right, a breeder must get a reasonable foal on the ground, have good people to handle it, grow it off without any major mistakes, and put it in good hands at the racetrack," Hancock said. "Then you have to have luck at every juncture."

By Frank Mitchell

Commercial Breeding Trends

With the exception of a handful of extremely wealthy owners, Thoroughbred breeders worldwide are focused on producing a commercial product. Even the wealthiest of owners must keep one eye on the auction markets because it's simply good business.

In 2005 more than $1.12 billion worth of Thoroughbred horses were sold in the United States and Canada, an all-time high for gross sales. Another $340.6 million were sold at major sales throughout Europe. What owner wouldn't pay attention to these numbers knowing it costs about $30,000 a year to keep one horse in training and the average racehorse in North America earned $16,177 in 2005? Most owners don't begin recouping their losses until they sell their horses as breeding stock or breed them and sell the offspring.

"Any owner realizes it is an expensive game, and they are good businessmen," said Garrett O'Rourke, farm manager at Juddmonte Farms, which is owned by Saudi Arabian businessman Khalid Abdullah. "They use good business practices and realize the benefit of keeping a certain amount of commercial bloodlines." Juddmonte has raced a lot of high-quality homebreds. In 2003 and 2004 the farm was the leading breeder of grade I winners in North America, having won with four each year. In 2005 it raced Breeders' Cup Filly and Mare Turf winner and champion turf female Intercontinental. The farm also sold more than $600,000 worth of broodmares that same year.

Commercial vs. Homebreds

Before discussing the relative value of commercial and homebred Thoroughbreds, we should first define what makes a Thoroughbred desirable.

Good conformation and an active family tree make a racing prospect valuable in the marketplace. A horse with good conformation is, generally speaking, well muscled, has good bone, and is straight through the knees. Also, the depth of its shoulder, the length of its midsection, and the length of its hip should be proportional to one another. An active family is one that is currently producing winners and stakes winners. A breeding prospect becomes even more valuable if it has a successful race record to go along with its good conformation and pedigree. A prime example is the champion racemare Ashado, who sold at the 2005 Keeneland November breeding stock sale for $9 million. She won 11 graded stakes, of which seven were grade I, and earned $3,261,440. Ashado is by the late Saint Ballado, who has sired 54 stakes winners, and is out of stakes winner Goulash, who has produced four other stakes-placed runners from six foals of racing age.

The matings that produce commercial horses are often influenced by changes in the market as much as by the recommendations of pedigree experts. A fashionably bred sale prospect typically derives its value from a popular but unproven first-generation pedigree. Any horse, however, must have decent conformation to have significant value at auction, and horses with fashionable pedigrees are no exception. Beyond that, the value of these horses is perceived value because they are often by young and unproven sires and/or are the first or second foals out of young mares. The breeding fees of stallions in their first two years at stud and the value of their first two crops both sell for a premium because the offspring have not had the chance to show whether they can run, so buyers err on the side of optimism.

It might be tempting to assume that horses bred to be sold are inferior to horses bred by the people who will race them and who also are keen on winning the biggest, most prestigious races. Homebreds do excel in some areas but certainly not all. To identify the differences, *The Blood-Horse MarketWatch* compiled the race records of all horses that raced in 2003, 2004, and 2005, and then compared the performance records of homebreds with the records of horses that were offered at some point through a public auction. The analysis showed that homebreds won the

ANNE M. EBERHARDT

El Prado sires runners that do well on both dirt and turf

highest percentages of stakes races, graded stakes, and grade I stakes among horses whose stud fees at conception were $15,000 or higher. Homebreds also had the highest average earnings and the highest percentages of horses earning $100,000 or more in six out of eight stud fee categories. *(See the chart on pages 88-89.)* The commercial runners, however, produced the highest percentages of two-year-old winners in six out of eight stud fee categories and were higher or equal to the homebreds in all stud fee categories by percentage of three-year-old winners. Horses offered at auction also had slightly higher overall percentages of stakes winners (7 percent for auction horses vs. 6 percent for homebreds) and graded stakes winners (1.7 percent vs. 1.1 percent). Homebreds fell behind in the overall statistics because significantly more homebreds were conceived on stud fees of $5,000 or less. The commercial horses had 14,159 runners in this category compared with 35,344 homebred runners. One consistent trend in both groups is that the least expensive horses, as judged by stud fee, were the poorest performers and earned the least amount of money on average.

While the debate about the superiority of homebreds versus commercial horses may never be fully answered, one thing is unquestionable: the commercial market is an important gateway that allows a greater number of people to participate in the industry.

"Everyone has a different niche, a different angle," said Michael Youngs, a bloodstock consultant in England, whose clients include Charlotte Weber's Live Oak Stud. In 2005, Live Oak won the Florida Derby with homebred High Fly. "Some buy the old mares no one wants anymore, and someone else is buying only young mares and breeding them to young stallions. This is good. If everyone in this industry was doing the same thing, the industry would collapse."

Breeding for the Commercial Market

The goal of every Thoroughbred breeder should be to produce a fast and durable racehorse, but like it or not, there are distinct differences between breeding for the commercial market versus breeding to race.

O'Rourke and Rob Keck, the pedigree expert at Crestwood Farm, both agreed that anyone breeding strictly for the commercial market needs to focus on young stock. Commercial market breeders need to buy broodmare prospects with good race records and breed them to young unproven sires.

"You are looking for a filly right out of racing or that is going to produce her first foal. There is no blot on her record," O'Rourke said. "If you have a mare that has a two-year-old and a yearling and a weanling, then there is high risk if she does not produce a runner (with that first foal). She will lose value." Grade I winner Hidden Lake, for example, probably would have sold for between $3 million and $4 million had she been sold in 1997 when she was retired from racing, O'Rourke said. Instead, she was bred and had produced two winners from three foals of racing age when she was first offered in foal to Sky Mesa at the 2004 Keeneland November sale. Hidden Lake was bought back for $425,000. She was offered again at the 2005 Fasig-

Tipton Kentucky November select sale and sold in foal to Distorted Humor for $525,000.

"There is a huge change in value based strictly on the commercial perception," O'Rourke said.

How did the offspring of unproven sires and mares become so valuable? Keck said buyers encouraged it.

"It used to be that people only bred young mares to proven sires," Keck said. "People would keep the mares and try to figure out who best to breed her to and get the best foal. Then when you produced a good runner and made her a stakes-producing mare, you could be proud of all the hard work. The people who used to police that were the buyers. They would not buy a young mare that was not bred to a proven sire, and now they don't care. When people stopped caring about those sorts of things, then they broke all the rules."

Keck said breeders who don't have a lot of money have to focus on getting a return. The best way to protect that return is to breed a young mare to a first-year stallion and sell her before she's had her second weanling.

"Second-crop weanlings lose so much value because the people buying them know that first crop of weanlings are now yearlings and when they are trying to pinhook the second crop, the first crop will be running and may not do very well." The first crop of weanlings by sires that entered stud in 2002, for example, sold for an average of $49,243 in 2003. The next year the

Stud Fee Ranges	*Commercial Runners*	*Commercial Winners*	*Wnrs (% Rnrs)*	*2YO Wnrs (% Rnrs)*	*3YO Wnrs (% Rnrs)*
$500,000-$100,000	455	372	372 (82%)	98 (22%)	259 (57%)
$90,000-$75,000	343	285	285 (83%)	63 (18%)	208 (61%)
$70,000-$50,000	943	837	837 (89%)	187 (20%)	532 (56%)
$48,000-$25,000	4,397	3,799	3,799 (86%)	1,075 (24%)	2,644 (60%)
$24,000-$15,000	4,508	3,956	3,956 (88%)	1,062 (24%)	2,751 (61%)
$14,600-$10,000	5,083	4,500	4,500 (89%)	1,289 (25%)	3,166 (62%)
$9,800-$5,000	9,733	8,434	8,434 (87%)	2,566 (26%)	6,031 (62%)
Less than $5,000	14,159	11,870	11,870 (84%)	3,611 (26%)	8,273 (58%)
All Horses	**39,621**	**34,053**	**34,053 (86%)**	**9,951 (25%)**	**23,864 (60%)**

Stud Fee Ranges	*Homebred Runners*	*Homebred Winners*	*Wnrs (% Rnrs)*	*2YO Wnrs (% Rnrs)*	*3YO Wnrs (% Rnrs)*
$500,000-$100,000	451	384	384 (85%)	90 (20%)	252 (56%)
$90,000-$75,000	207	172	172 (83%)	39 (19%)	118 (57%)
$70,000-$50,000	487	424	424 (87%)	78 (16%)	266 (55%)
$48,000-$25,000	1,860	1,610	1,610 (87%)	360 (19%)	1,120 (60%)
$24,000-$15,000	2,076	1,814	1,814 (87%)	384 (18%)	1,235 (59%)
$14,600-$10,000	2,854	2,443	2,443 (86%)	542 (19%)	1,711 (60%)
$9,800-$5,000	7,786	6,632	6,632 (85%)	1,581 (20%)	4,571 (59%)
Less than $5,000	35,344	28,008	28,008 (79%)	5,267 (15%)	17,354 (49%)
All Horses	**51,065**	**41,487**	**41,487 (81%)**	**8,341 (16%)**	**26,627 (52%)**

value of weanlings by these sires slid to $36,763.

Breeders also looking at the commercial market should avoid sires that ran primarily on the grass, according to O'Rourke and Keck. Turf sires are certainly capable of producing runners that can perform equally well on grass and dirt — El Prado is a good example — but there is a prejudice in most buyers' minds about turf. The prejudice is rooted in the reality that North America offers a limited number of turf races.

"Instead of running every three or four weeks, you run every six or seven just because there are not opportunities," O'Rourke said. "If you have a dirt horse and a track doesn't have a race with the right conditions, you can always find an opportunity somewhere else. At the end of a year, a dirt horse will make three or four more starts than the turf horse."

Keck said he understands the turf bias but believes turf sires get knocked unfairly on two counts. First, he believes people pay too much attention to the sire side of a pedigree, and secondly, most stallions that produce top turf runners also can produce top dirt runners. Keck bred a filly named Princess Pelona, who was by El Prado and out of Peachtree City (by Carson City). The filly is a stakes winner on dirt. Her added-money victories include the 2006 Snow Goose Stakes, worth $75,000 at Laurel Park. She also has placed in two allowance races on the grass out of four turf starts. Princess Pelona's

4YO Wnrs (% Rnrs)	*SWs (% Rnrs)*	*GSWs (% Rnrs)*	*G1SWs (% Rnrs)*	*Gross Earnings Commercial*	*Avg Earnings Commercial*	*$100k+ Earners (% Rnrs)*
182 (40%)	77 (17%)	34 (7.5%)	8 (1.8%)	$44,501,207	$97,805	122 (27%)
147 (43%)	46 (13%)	18 (5.2%)	5 (1.5%)	$29,481,916	$85,953	85 (25%)
564 (60%)	109 (12%)	49 (5.2%)	12 (1.3%)	$90,519,630	$95,991	232 (25%)
2,100 (48%)	416 (9%)	149 (3.4%)	30 (0.7%)	$356,168,588	$81,003	934 (21%)
2,605 (58%)	350 (8%)	98 (2.2%)	24 (0.5%)	$347,186,150	$77,016	998 (22%)
2,834 (56%)	408 (8%)	108 (2.1%)	23 (0.5%)	$374,248,547	$73,627	1,030 (20%)
5,350 (55%)	620 (6%)	112 (1.2%)	32 (0.3%)	$637,518,622	$65,501	1,841 (19%)
7,763 (55%)	890 (6%)	91 (0.6%)	27 (0.2%)	$738,186,542	$52,135	1,964 (14%)
1,545 (54%)	**2,916 (7%)**	**659 (1.7%)**	**161 (0.4%)**	**$2,617,811,202**	**$66,071**	**7,206 (18%)**

4YO Wnrs (% Rnrs)	*SWs (% Rnrs)*	*GSWs (% Rnrs)*	*G1SWs (% Rnrs)*	*Gross Earnings Homebred*	*Avg Earnings Homebred*	*$100k+ Earners (% Rnrs)*
224 (50%)	86 (19%)	45 (10%)	17 (3.8%)	$62,215,837	$137,951	149 (33%)
101 (49%)	34 (16%)	17 (8.2%)	6 (2.9%)	$28,534,526	$137,848	62 (30%)
315 (65%)	66 (14%)	27 (5.5%)	8 (1.6%)	$55,879,631	$114,743	144 (30%)
988 (53%)	211 (11%)	76 (4.1%)	22 (1.2%)	$176,559,591	$94,925	481 (26%)
,251 (60%)	203 (10%)	59 (2.8%)	19 (0.9%)	$188,621,509	$90,858	524 (25%)
,603 (56%)	234 (8%)	64 (2.2%)	22 (0.8%)	$221,827,259	$77,725	610 (21%)
4,298 (55%)	509 (7%)	111 (1.4%)	34 (0.4%)	$493,786,991	$63,420	1,350 (17%)
9,935 (56%)	1,884 (5%)	166 (0.5%)	56 (0.2%)	$1,503,515,206	$42,539	3,695 (10%)
8,715 (56%)	**3,227 (6%)**	**565 (1.1%)**	**184 (0.4%)**	**$2,730,940,551**	**$53,480**	**7,015 (14%)**

career earnings totaled $321,615 after the Snow Goose.

During the 2005 Keeneland September yearling sale, Crestwood Farm tried to sell a Lear Fan half brother to Princess Pelona.

"Everyone that looked at the horse saw Lear Fan and thought, 'This is a turf horse with stamina.' They didn't ask anything about the mare," Keck said. At the time of the sale, Princess Pelona was only stakes-placed. Being by Carson City, Princess Pelona has plenty of speed in her pedigree. Her first stakes win was at seven furlongs, and her second was at a mile.

"If you printed her pedigree with the mare on top, then everyone would have looked at it and thought, 'This is all speed. Carson City is speed. This is going to be a precocious two-year-old.' I bred the mare to Lear Fan to have a horse with some stamina that wasn't a total speedball." The Lear Fan colt was eventually withdrawn from the sale.

The use of Polytrack as a racing surface could change appreciably turf sires' reputation. Polytrack is a synthetic surface made of blended ground rubber and wax-coated sand.

"It is in between dirt and turf," O'Rourke said. "Dirt horses like it and turf horses do well on it. It is an equalizer."

In 2005 the Northern Kentucky racetrack Turfway Park became the first racing facility in the United States to install Polytrack on its main track. The California Horse Racing Commission has since decided to have Polytrack installed on all its major racetracks over the next several years. Woodbine near Toronto also will install Polytrack.

"The perception at Turfway is that horses that had raced on grass had come over and raced very effectively on it," O'Rourke said. "If they race effectively and they bring in more Polytrack racing, we'll see more interest in turf pedigrees."

Breeding To Race

Time is on the side of owners who breed to race. They don't need a foal by a hot young sire so they can sell it quickly, and they don't necessarily need a horse that comes out blazing as a two-year-old in order to begin generating revenue.

"Where we don't have to pay attention [to the commercial market] is if we see an absolutely perfect mating that a commercial breeder would not consider under any circumstances," O'Rourke said. "What means more to us is balancing having a good commercial horse and a good racehorse, and with us the racehorse always comes first."

For example, Juddmonte has also used Lear Fan effectively, according to O'Rourke. The farm bred and raced Ryafan, who is Lear Fan's leading runner to date by career earnings. In 1997 she was champion grass mare in the United States and champion three-year-old filly in Europe. Ryafan won four grade/group I races out of 10 starts and earned $1,345,140.

"Most breeders ignored Lear Fan for a number of reasons," O'Rourke said. "For one, his appearance. He was a big, strong, but plain-looking horse. He was also a grass horse, which is uncommercial. Once a stallion hits 10 years of age, he may still produce runners, but the gloss goes off of him. You can see that in the number of mares they breed. It is a marvel how stallions that have really done nothing wrong but didn't have that big horse, you see their fees drop and the numbers of mares bred go down."

Dynaformer is another sire who, early in his stud career, was an owner/breeder sire with limited commercial appeal. The reason, according to Keck, is that he tends to sire ugly horses "that look goofy, but they can run." Now the Three Chimneys Farm stallion is used by predominantly rich owner/breeders and has developed into a commercially viable sire. But, in 2006, one of Dynaformer's top performers was a homebred — his grade I-winning son Barbaro.

When selecting mares for an owner/breeder operation, O'Rourke said breedability and soundness are essential.

"Obviously a mare like Ashado is very desirable from a racing point of view and a breeding point of view, but these kinds of mares don't come along all that frequently. There are things you can overlook. You may have a mare that has never been bred to a really good stallion and still may have runners with 20 starts apiece. I love a mare like that."

Keck said the perfect broodmare is the one that has produced the highest percentage of winners among whatever mares the buyer can afford.

"Your stallion selection could be commercial or not commercial," Keck said. "But on the broodmare side, people are fooling themselves if they don't have black type there. When you have a yearling with three blank dams [no black type] on the catalog page, then you have a non-commercial broodmare and the chance of her producing a stakes winner is slim."

A broodmare also doesn't have to have a race record to be a worthwhile investment, according to Keck.

"I would rather have the unraced mare that is related to two other mares that raced and produced stakes winners than to have a stakes winner with no other runners in the family," he said.

The biggest mistake that breeders make when shopping for a mare, according to Keck, is not having an idea of whom they will breed her to if they buy her. An even bigger mistake is made when broodmare buyers acquire a mare that has a similar pedigree to a hot sire.

"[Broodmare buyers] will say they love Distorted Humor, so they buy a mare by Forty Niner (the sire of Distorted Humor) — wrong," Keck said. Most pedigree people are not doing tail-male line inbreeding, meaning the sire's sire or grandsire is within the first three generations on both the sire side and dam side of the pedigree. But, Keck said, this is getting harder and harder to avoid. He said the pedigree of Jump Start is a good example. Within the first three generations on both sides of this sire's pedigree are A.P. Indy, Seattle Slew, Storm Cat, Mr. Prospector, and Secretariat. Jump Start is a sire in search of an outcross.

"I'm an inbreeding guy, but you don't want to be the one to breed 3x3 to Mr. Prospector," Keck said. "You need to find the families that cross well with those hot sires. If you find a mare that you like, go do the research, do a hypothetical mating, and find out if you can get to the horse and if it is affordable. And I try to figure out who to breed her to for more than one year. No one does that."

Finally, Keck recommends that you find a mare with some size because most stallions are medium-sized in height. He said Tiznow is a "breath of fresh air" because he is such a big stallion (16.3 hands). Not many stallions with big and lengthy bodies have been successful because their foals tend to mature later and prefer longer distances. These types of foals generally don't have the precocious speed that most American buyers want in a racing prospect. The big stallions that have been successes include Roberto and his son Kris S., both of whom proved to be sires of sires. Roberto, who is by Hail to Reason, has been so successful he is considered the head of his own sire line that also includes Dynaformer, Lear Fan, Red Ransom, and Silver Hawk. Kris S. sired 1989 Breeders' Cup Turf winner Prized, who in turn sired Brass Hat, winner of the 2006 Donn Handicap and runner-up in the Dubai World Cup.

In Tiznow's case, the partnership of WinStar and Taylor Made Farm planned well by giving preference in his first book to mares that had raced at two or had foals that developed early. Their strategy paid off, and Tiznow became the leading freshman sire of 2006. His top first-crop runner was Folklore, juvenile filly champion of 2006 and winner of the Breeders' Cup Juvenile Fillies.

Whether breeding for the commercial market or breeding to race, no one can ignore the importance of quality. A horse with a dazzling pedigree and poor conformation has little commercial value. A horse with good conformation but few winners in the immediate family is a longshot to be a star at the track.

A pedigree analysis by pedigree researcher Avalyn Hunter of mares that had produced at least two grade/group I winners in a given year confirmed that top racehorses beget top racehorses. The study, which appeared in the April 16, 2004, issue of *The Blood-Horse MarketWatch*, compared the grade and/or group I producers with a random group of dams born between 1963 and 1990. The elite producers were much better racehorses overall. They included four champions, seven graded stakes winners, and eight non-graded stakes winners compared with the random group that included only one group I winner and one stakes-placed runner. The elite producers also had stronger pedigrees, with more grade/group I winners in their five-generation pedigrees than the random group, and were part of families that showed great consistency in producing black-type winners.

Pedigree experts emphasize that broodmare buyers must buy the best pedigree and conformation they can afford. Then when breeders are choosing the stallion, it is important for them to keep the commercial market in mind but essential to study the crosses that have already proven to be successful. Breeding is a game of percentages so put the odds in your favor.

By Eric Mitchell

PART III

Veterinary Overview

Pre-Breeding Mare and Stallion Care

The birth of a live, healthy foal begins well in advance of transporting the mare to the stallion. The mare first should be in good physical and reproductive health. In essence, her body should be fine-tuned for both conception and carrying a foal to term.

A portion of the preparation should be ongoing, featuring a proper immunization program, regular deworming, and a balanced diet that allows her to be healthy and robust, but neither overly fat nor overly thin. Then before the breeding season, a veterinarian should examine her to determine her reproductive capability.

We will examine these aspects of general health and reproductive efficiency with help from a wide variety of sources. Much of the information will be drawn from research conducted at Colorado State University, Texas A&M University and the University of Minnesota.

Having a broodmare in sound breeding condition is important because mares are not the most reproductively efficient animals in the world. Wild horses have between a 50 percent and 60 percent conception rate, depending on the harshness of their environment and the food supply. Man has increased that percentage in well-managed breeding operations, but it is far from perfect. One study of a large group of Thoroughbred mares found that 77.9 percent of the mares conceived and 69.7 percent had foals that lived beyond six weeks.

The study also showed that age is a factor. Mares under nine years of age had a conception rate of 82.6 percent. Mares 10 to 13 years of age had a conception rate of 78.9 percent while mares over 14 years of age had a conception rate of 74.4 percent. The underlying message here is that producing foals over a span of time produces wear and tear on the reproductive system, especially the uterus.

One equine reproduction specialist estimates that 20 percent to 25 percent of older mares fall into the "problem breeder" category compared to 2 percent or 3 percent for maiden mares.

Fertility

Figuring prominently in the equation is reproductive health. Numerous studies have shown that mares with no history of reproductive problems are the most fertile.

As indicated above, the first step toward good reproductive health involves keeping the mare free of disease and on a sound nutritional program. The immunization program will vary geographically, but generally all mares should be vaccinated against western and eastern encephalomyelitis and against West Nile virus. Science has pretty well settled that the once controversial West Nile vaccines are safe for pregnant mares. The broodmare also should be current on tetanus shots, and a flu vaccine might be warranted. Once she is pregnant, the mare should be protected against diseases that can cause her to abort, such as rhinopneumonitis.

Nutrition

Proper nutrition is highly important. Obese mares and overly thin mares often do not have high conception rates. The ideal is somewhere in between. If one uses body scores that range from one to nine, with one being overly thin and nine being obese, the ideal score would be five for a mare being prepared for breeding.

A nutritional program aimed at achieving a body score of five can vary from mare to mare. For some, it might involve a diet of high-quality alfalfa hay only; for others, it might mean that hay and a grain supplement are required. Consult with your veterinarian for your mare's optimal nutrition needs.

Regardless of the diet, the mare's nutritional health can be compromised if internal parasites are not controlled. This is handled through a varied but consistent deworming program. That program will vary geographically and should be designed with a veterinarian's input.

Light

The mare's reproductive system reawakens in the spring when days lengthen. As the mare's brain records increased light and higher temperatures, the hypothalamus gland, located within tissues of the mid-brain, is stimulated. It signals the start up of the reproductive system by producing a gonadotropic releasing hormone (GnRH). When

ANNE M. EBERHARDT

Every breeder's goal: a healthy mare and foal

GnRH is secreted in the appropriate quantity, the pituitary gland, located at the base of the brain, is stimulated. The pituitary gland then secretes two hormones that affect the ovaries. The first hormone is known as follicle stimulating hormone (FSH). It travels along the bloodstream to the ovaries, where it stimulates development of one or more follicles.

The follicles, when they reach 20 to 25 millimeters in diameter, secrete estrogen. This hormone stimulates estrual activity, causes relaxation of the cervix, stimulates contractions along the mare's reproductive tract, and signals the pituitary gland to cease secretion of FSH, and, at the same time, stimulates release of the second gonadotropic hormone — luteinizing hormone (LH).

The luteinizing hormone facilitates maturation and ovulation of the growing, egg-bearing follicle. Ovulation occurs when the mature egg leaves the follicle and begins its trip through the oviduct. In the wake of ovulation, the estrogen level falls and the remains of the ovulated follicle are converted to form a corpus luteum (CL) or yellow body. The luteal cells secrete the hormone progesterone. It is the job of progesterone to shut down the estrus-stimulating hormones to set the stage for maintaining a pregnancy.

And, it all began with light. To make certain that the mare's reproductive system reawakens on cue, artificial light can be used as a stimulant. Normally, one would expose the mare to artificial lights for 16 hours per day eight to 10 weeks prior to the projected breeding season. Most mares exposed to light stimulation of that duration will begin to cycle sometime within the eight- to 10-week period. The rule of thumb is that a 200-watt light bulb in a 12x12-foot stall will provide an appropriate amount of light for stimulation.

Pre-Breeding Exam

Now that the mare is in good health, has received her immunizations, and has been exposed to light, it is time to determine whether a physical problem or problems will prevent her from conceiving. It is time for a veterinarian to do a pre-breeding exam.

Before that occurs, however, the mare owner should have given long and serious thought to whether the mare is an appropriate candidate for reproduction. Does she have correct conformation that appropriately represents the Thoroughbred breed? Conformational characteristics very often are passed on from generation to generation. Perhaps equally important is the mare's temperament. Research indicates that high-strung, nervous mares suffer from higher abortion rates due to their high stress levels, which, in turn, elevate cortisol levels; higher cortisol levels can disrupt the normal reproductive endocrine control mechanisms.

There is also the practical aspect that involves ease of handling. The aggressive, nervous mare may become highly agitated when a stallion approaches her. Temperament, too, is a heritable trait, and a high-strung, nervous mare is apt to produce a high-strung, nervous offspring. In addition, foals often mirror the attitudes and actions of their dams. Thus, it is something of double jeopardy — heredity and environment combined in a negative way.

Mare History

Step number one in a pre-breeding exam is for the owner to provide the mare's complete history to the examining veterinarian. Included should be information on her last foaling date, the number of services before she became pregnant, a complete report on her last foaling (was it difficult or normal), a rundown on any physical problems, dietary needs, and weight changes, as well as information on her vaccination and deworming schedule.

This background will likely help the veterinarian understand problems that might show up during the breeding soundness examination. With the mare's history in hand, the veterinarian can conduct a visual examination.

This exam can provide clues as to whether the mare is a prime candidate for infection of the reproductive tract. For example, a high croup and high tailset indicate a mare could be prone to bacterial invasions of the reproductive tract as fecal material falls against her vagina when she defecates.

When this is the case, a Caslick's procedure might be performed in the wake of conception. With this approach, sutures are used to close off most of the vagina, with an opening left at the bottom to allow for the excretion of urine.

Internal Examination

Once the visual examination is complete, the veterinarian will perform a physical exam using an ultrasound machine, a lighted instrument called a speculum, rectal palpation, or a combination.

Ultrasound has the capability of identifying endometrial cysts, fibrous masses, fluid, uterine tumors, ovarian tumors, ovarian hematomas, and ovarian cysts. When problems, such as cysts, are identified, the practitioner must decide whether they will compro-

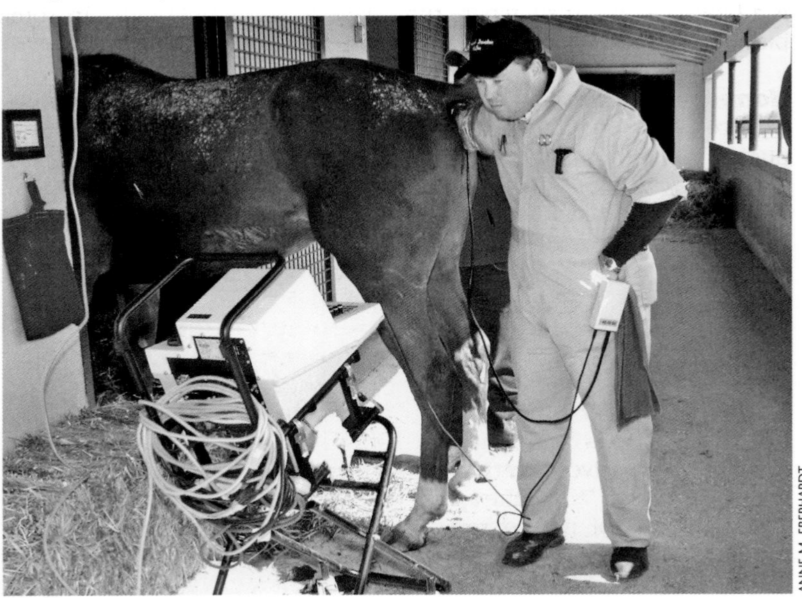
ANNE M. EBERHARDT

Palpating a mare

mise the mare's ability to become pregnant and carry a foal to term. If this is the case, a treatment program might be called for.

Additional Approaches

Following are some additional approaches the veterinarian might employ to determine breeding soundness in the mare:

Endometrial culture: This involves a general evaluation of the bacterial status of the uterine lumen.

Cytology: This involves studying slide samples under the microscope.

Endometrial biopsy: In this procedure, small samples of uterine tissue are retrieved and studied.

Hysteroscopy: This involves using a flexible fiberoptiscope to visualize the structure within the uterus.

Tubal patency: This procedure involves flushing a dye through the oviducts to determine if there is a blockage and, if so, where the blockage occurs.

Hormonal Assessment

Once the mare has been thoroughly examined both externally and internally, it is time for a hormonal assessment. Earlier we mentioned the important role of progesterone in maintaining a pregnancy. Progesterone's initial task is to subdue the actively contracting reproductive tract and to tighten and close the relaxed and open cervix. It also prohibits the secretion of FSH and LH from the pituitary, thus effectively putting the mare out of heat. When the appropriate amount of progesterone is produced, all of the above happen in proper order. However, not all mares secrete the appropriate amount of progesterone.

The good news is that progesterone levels can be monitored and supplemental progesterone can be administered. However, if a progesterone dysfunction is not determined early on, the mare might go through a number of estrous cycles without maintaining a pregnancy.

Teasing

Once it has been determined that the mare is a viable candidate for breeding and she has been placed under lights, it is time to begin the teasing procedure. The importance of teasing cannot be over-emphasized, with a number of researchers maintaining that lack of an appropriate teasing program figures prominently in low pregnancy rates.

Major breeding establishments use stallions other than those involved in covering mares in the teasing process. At smaller operations, the breeding stallion might have to do double duty. In some instances, the teasing is conducted one on one. In others, the stallion might be placed in an enclosure or "cage" in the midst of a group of mares. The theory in the latter case is that mares coming into estrus will approach the enclosure and demonstrate their willingness to be bred. The more effective approach, it would appear, would be one on one, with a barrier between stallion and mare to prevent injury.

Edward L. Squires, PhD, of Colorado State University, has made this statement about teasing: "Inadequate or improper teasing constitutes a major cause of poor reproduction performance in mares. Normally, cycling mares should be teased daily with at least one stallion. Mares that have not

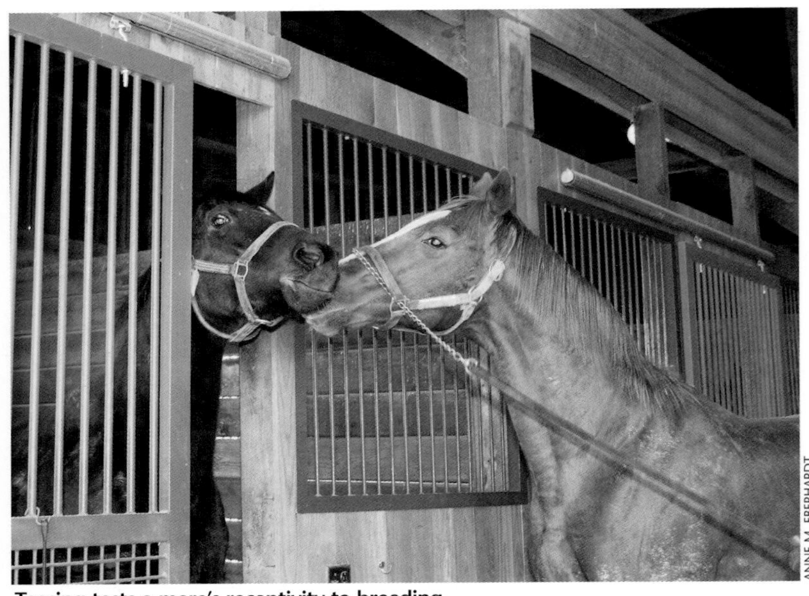
ANNE M. EBERHARDT

Teasing tests a mare's receptivity to breeding

achieved normal cycles and mares exhibiting the first day of diestrus [stage of a mare's cycle in which a corpus luteum forms and progesterone production increases] should be teased with two stallions. The mare should be teased by the stallion head to head, at the buttocks and external genitalia."

Mares that are ready to be bred will normally squat, urinate, and allow the stallion to nuzzle them.

It is important that the teasing process is not hurried. It has been suggested that in group teasing, mares need 15 to 20 minutes to demonstrate their behavior. In hand teasing, several minutes should be spent with each mare.

Pregnancy Check

The next step is breeding the mare. (With Thoroughbreds, it must be by natural cover.) Thanks to ultrasound, a pregnancy can be determined very shortly after breeding. Some practitioners conduct the first ultrasound examination for pregnancy 14 days after breeding — some even earlier.

In some cases, the ultrasound exam will reveal not only that the mare is pregnant but also that she will have twins. This is considered to be a problem as the health of at least one of the twins often is compromised.

The normal procedure at days 14 to 16 days of twin pregnancy is to crush or "pinch off" one of the vesicles. The veterinarian will do this either with his or her fingers or with the transducer of the ultrasound unit.

Along the way during pregnancy, the mare's progesterone levels should be monitored regularly. If the mare has a history of problems during pregnancy, the veterinarian must be most vigilant in monitoring all hormonal levels and must take all necessary protective procedures, such as Caslick's. Many of the potential problems will have surfaced during the pre-breeding examination, providing the veterinarian with advance knowledge concerning the potential for trouble.

The Stallion

Obviously, the stallion plays a key role in reproduction, and his reproductive good health is as important to a successful pregnancy as is the health of the mare. As with the mare, proper nutrition, appropriate immunizations, regular deworming, good dental care, and appropriate hoof trimming figure into the equation. Also highly important is exercise. A stallion that enters the breeding season overweight and with little muscle tone just might be an inefficient breeder. The exercise regimen might involve routine turnout or riding or both.

A pre-breeding examination of the stallion is highly important. It should begin with a history of the horse's past performance in the breeding shed. Texas A&M University researchers Dickson Varner, DVM, MS, and Terry Blanchard, DVM, MS, have listed seven areas for which specific information should be sought on the potential breeding stallion:

- Number of mares bred and number pregnant.
- Frequency of breeding. This should include the number of mares bred daily as well as in the previous week.
- Number of services per cycle.
- Pregnancy rate per cycle.
- Cumulative pregnancy rate for season.
- Pertinent information concerning mares, including the number of maiden, lactating, and barren mares bred, with respective pregnancy rates for each group.
- Sexual behavior. Does the stallion fully insert the penis into the vagina, remain mounted until ejaculation occurs, and show positive evidence of ejaculation (such as sperm present in dismount sam-

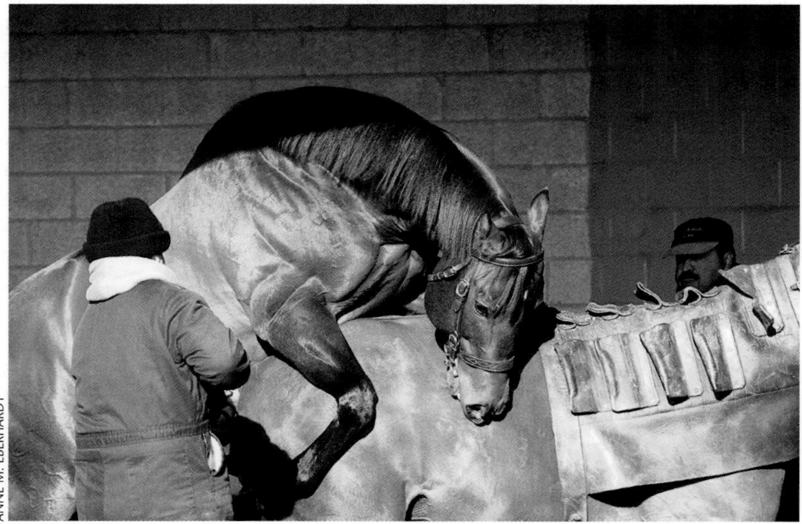
ANNE M. EBERHARDT

A stallion should have a strong libido or desire to breed

ple) during copulation?

After studying the stallion's history, the next step is a complete physical examination, including the genitalia. Of particular interest is the size of the stallion's testicles because testicular size correlates with daily sperm production — the larger the testicles, in most cases, the higher the sperm production.

Also of importance is the stallion's libido. Unless the stallion has a desire to breed, his sperm production is of little consequence. Libido is determined by observing the stallion's reaction when presented to a mare in heat. A stallion with appropriate libido will become sexually aroused quickly.

Once the physical examination is concluded, it is time to collect semen and make a sperm count. Total sperm number in an ejaculate is subject to seasonal variation but also is affected by numerous other factors, including frequency of ejaculation, age, testicular size and sperm production capability, size of extragonadal sperm reserves, and various types of reproductive disease.

Total number of sperm in stallion ejaculates typically ranges from 2 to 3 billion to 20 billion. Young stallions bred with frequency often are on the lower end of the scale while mature stallions bred infrequently are on the upper end. There is another factor that figures into the equation — sperm motility. (Sperm "motility" is described as sperm exhibiting motility of any form while "progressive sperm motility" describes sperm that are moving in a rapid linear manner.) It is generally believed that vigorous sperm motility provides a strong assist in obtaining a pregnancy.

Still another aspect of sperm health to be checked involves the presence of morphological characteristics, such as deformities. Generally speaking, a high number of sperm defects can translate into lower fertility.

Conclusion

Thorough pre-breeding examinations for both stallions and mares are highly valuable. First, it might eliminate some as candidates for the reproductive process. Second, the examinations might reveal problems that can be handled and controlled with appropriately designed and timed procedures that will allow a mare to become pregnant and carry the foal to term despite some reproductive shortcomings.

By Les Sellnow

Frequently Asked Questions

How do you obtain a mare?

The most common ways to obtain a mare are at public auction, in a private transaction, or from a claiming race at the track.

How much should I expect to pay?

Mares, both in foal and not in foal, and broodmare prospects come in all price ranges. At public auction, mares can sell anywhere from $1,000 to millions of dollars. Claiming prices for fillies and mares range from $1,500 to $150,000.

Where do I keep my mare?

Unless you own a farm and have the facilities to care for a mare and her foal, you can keep your mare at a boarding facility. Many farms specialize in boarding mares and are equipped to manage your mare, handle foaling, and raise the foal.

What are some of the costs associated with owning a mare?

In addition to the purchase price and stud fees, you can expect to pay monthly boarding fees (approximately $30 a day at a good Kentucky farm, or $11,000 a year). You also will pay insurance premiums, and routine veterinary, farrier, and dentistry bills (up to $2,000 a year). Vanning costs to and from the breeding shed can range from $125 to $200.

Sometimes complications can occur during pregnancy and delivery which will result in additional veterinary bills. Once the foal arrives, you will pay for its care, which usually is less than the mare's board. You also will pay insurance (if desired), veterinary, and farrier bills for the foal and additional costs associated with sales preparation if the foal is destined for the auction ring.

Are there tax advantages to mare ownership and breeding?

There can be tax advantages associated with ownership if you operate your program as a business. Generally, horses can be depreciated over three to seven years, depending on age. Each state and the federal government treat ownership differently. If you intend to operate as a business you need to have defined goals and a business plan. It's best to seek advice from a Thoroughbred tax professional.

How do I choose the best stallion for my mare?

There are several considerations which can vary depending on the outcome you hope to achieve. If your sole intention is to race the resultant foal, then your primary consideration should be to select a stallion that suits the mare and has the ability to produce a quality runner. If your intention is to sell the resultant foal, then you have to consider the above as well as some other factors. The quality of the mare generally will dictate the type of stallion you choose. You do not want to "overbreed" or "underbreed" your mare. An adviser or reputable farm manager can help you decide.

How soon can I expect a return on my investment?

If you buy an in-foal mare at a fall breeding stock sale, you can conceivably sell the offspring as a weanling at the following year's breeding stock sale. If you sell the offspring as a yearling, you will have to wait until the year after the foal's birth. If you are breeding to race, you will have to wait at least two years for that foal to make it to the races. There is no guarantee, however, that you will recoup your investment in the sales ring or at the track.

Where can I find a reputable advisor?

The Greatest Game, a program that matches new and prospective owners with an agent, is a good place to start (www.thegreatestgame.com). In addition, you can contact the Thoroughbred Owners and Breeders Association (www.toba.org), your state association, or farm managers of prominent horse farms in your area for help in locating advisers.

ANNE M. EBERHARDT

Some farms specialize in boarding mares and foals

Glossary

Agent — a person who has the authority to conduct business for another: for example, to buy or sell a horse.

Back at the knee — describes a horse's leg that appears to have a backward or concave arc, with the center of the arc at the knee when viewed in profile.

Barren — a term used to describe a mare that was bred during a breeding season but did not conceive.

Base narrow — describes a horse that has feet that are closer together than the hocks and thighs.

Bay — a color classification that ranges from light tan to dark brown and marked by a black mane and tail and by black points on the legs (with the exception of any white markings).

Biomechanics — the study of the mechanics of a living body, especially of the forces exerted by muscles and gravity on the skeletal structure.

Black type — a sales catalog designation for stakes winners and stakes-placed horses. Stakes winners are designated by bold-faced capital letters while stakes-placed horses are bold-faced. Not all stakes races are eligible for black-type designation.

Blood typing — a method of verifying a horse's parentage and is required by The Jockey Club to register a horse.

Bloodlines — a horse's pedigree.

Bloodstock agent — a person who specializes in buying and selling horses, breeding seasons, and stallion shares.

Book — n. the group of mares bred to a stallion in a given year; v. the act of signing a contract to breed a mare to a stallion.

Bottom line — a term used to refer to a horse's female family (the bottom line of the pedigree).

Bred — a horse is considered bred at the place of its birth (e.g., state, country).

Breeder — the owner of the broodmare at the time she foals.

Breeding farm — a Thoroughbred farm used for breeding and raising potential racehorses.

Breeding right — the right to breed a mare to a stallion for one or more breeding seasons, but usually does not include an ownership interest in the stallion.

Breeding soundness exam — physical examination performed on a mare by a veterinarian for the purposes of determining her breeding health.

Broodmare — a mare that has been bred and is used for

breeding purposes.

Broodmare prospect — a filly or mare that has not yet been bred but is capable of being used for breeding purposes.

Broodmare sire — the dam's sire in a pedigree line.

Buy-back — a horse offered at public auction that did not meet its reserve bid was, therefore, not sold.

Cannon bone — the bone between the knee or hock and the fetlock (ankle). A common site of fracture in racehorses.

Champion — in the United States, a horse that receives an Eclipse Award via votes from eligible members of the National Thoroughbred Racing Association, the National Turf Writers Association, and the *Daily Racing Form*.

Chestnut — a color classification that ranges from gold to red to near brown. A chestnut horse will not have a black mane, tail, or points on its legs.

Claiming race — a race in which each horse entered is eligible to be purchased at a set price.

Classics — in the United States, the Kentucky Derby, Preakness Stakes, and Belmont Stakes, which comprise the Triple Crown.

Colt — an ungelded (entire) male horse up to four years of age.

Conditions of Sale — the legal terms that govern how an auction is conducted. They are usually found in the sale catalog and might be announced by the auctioneer prior to the sale.

Conformation — the way horse is put together physically.

Cover — a single breeding of a mare to a stallion.

Cow-hocked — describes a horse whose hocks appear close together with the feet spread apart.

Cribber — a horse that habitually latches onto an object with its teeth and swallows or sucks air. Considered an undesirable stable vice.

Dam — a horse's mother.

Dark bay/brown — a color classification that ranges from deep brown to a dark brown that almost appears black. Brown hair will be found on the muzzle, flank, inner forearms, or thighs.

Dosage — a mathematical computation based on pedigree that Thoroughbred breeders use to classify a horse's ability to run certain distances.

DNA testing — a newer method of determining a Thoroughbred's parentage and is now being implementing by The Jockey Club.

Dual hemisphere breeding — the practice of standing a stallion for the breeding season in the Northern Hemisphere (February to July), then sending him to stand the Southern Hemisphere breeding season (August to December).

Fetlock — the joint between the cannon bone and the long pastern bone; also called the ankle.

Filly — a female horse up to age four year that has never been bred.

Foal — n. a baby horse that has not yet been weaned from its mother; v. the act of a broodmare giving birth.

Foal heat — the first time a mare comes into season after giving birth.

Foal sharing — an arrangement between the owner of a stallion share or season and the owner of a broodmare to breed them and to share the foal(s) by either owning half-interest in the foal or owning every other foal the broodmare produces.

Full brother (sister) — a male (female) horse that has the same sire and dam as other horses.

Get — progeny; usually refers to a stallion's offspring.

Granddam — the second dam of a horse.

Grandsire — the father of a horse's sire.

Gray/Roan — a color classification recognized by The Jockey Club. Gray horses have a mixture of white hair with their base color (bay, chestnut, etc.) but become more and more white as they age. Roan horses also have a mix of white hair with a base color, but they stay the same color throughout their life.

Half brother (sister) — a male (female) horses that has the same dam as other horses but a different sire.

Hand — the unit of measurement for a horse's height. Each hand equals four inches. A horse's height is measured from the ground to the withers.

Heterozygous — two different copies of the same gene, with one copy being inherited from each parent.

Homozygous — both copies of the gene inherited from each parent are the same.

Horse — any ungelded male five years old or older.

Inbreeding — having one or more common ancestors within the first five generations.

In foal — when a mare is pregnant.

In-foal guarantee — in a breeding contract, the stud fee is due on predetermined date and is not returnable once the mare is pregnant

The Jockey Club — the governing body for Thoroughbred breeding and racing.

Live foal guarantee — in a breeding contract, the stud fee is returned or, if not yet paid, is void if the mare does not get pregnant, aborts, or delivers a sickly foal that cannot stand and nurse. Sometimes the stud fee is due in the fall of the pregnancy and sometimes it is due when the foal stands and nurses.

Linebreeding — having one or more common ancestors beyond the first five generations

Maiden — a female horse that has never been bred; also a horse that has never won a race; also a type of race open to horses that have never won a race.

Mare — a female horse five years old or older or a younger female horse that has been bred.

Nick — a breeding theory based on the affinity of one bloodline for another.

No guarantee — in a breeding contract, the mare owner assumes all the risk and must pay the stud fee regardless of whether the mare gets pregnant

Offset knees — describes a horse whose forearm and cannon bone don't align.

Outcross — having no common ancestors within the first five generations.

Over at the knee — describes a horse's leg that has a forward or convex appearance at the knee when viewed from the side.

Palpation — the physical examination of a mare to feel or "palpate" her ovaries and uterus to determine breeding soundness, readiness to breed, uterine condition, pregnancy.

Pastern — the area between the fetlock joint and the hoof.

Pedigree — a horse's family tree, listing all the horse's ancestors by generation.

Produce record — a list of a mare's offspring.

Producer — a broodmare who has offspring that have won on the racetrack.

Repository — the area on the sales grounds where X-rays and other medical information are kept for inspection by buyers and veterinarians.

RNA — "reserve not attained"; the letters are used in sales results to indicate that a horse did not meet its reserve price.

Ridgeling — a male horse that has one or both testes undescended; also called a cryptorchid.

Select sale — a sale that is limited to horses chosen on pedigree and conformation.

Sickle-hocked — describes a horse whose cannon bones that are placed forward and under its hips,

Sire — a horse's father.

Sire line — in a pedigree, the line of stallions from generation to generation.

Slipped — a term used to describe a mare that aborted her foal.

Sound — a term used to describe a hose that is free from injury.

Stakes producer — a broodmare who has offspring that have won stakes races.

Stallion — a male horse used for breeding.

Stallion prospect — a male horse that is capable of being used for breeding purposes.

Stallion season — the right to mate a mare to a stallion during one breeding year.

Stallion share — a proprietary interesting a stallion, giving the owner the right to breed a mare to a stallion every breeding season for as long as the share is owned or to sell that right to another.

Straight behind — describes a horse whose hind legs, when viewed from the side, do not have much angle between the thigh bone (femur) and tibia.

Stud — a male horse used for breeding; also a breeding farm.

Stud book — the registry and genealogical record of the Thoroughbred breed, maintained by The Jockey Club.

Stud fee — the fee paid by a mare owner for the right to breed a mare to a stallion during a certain breeding period.

Suckling — a young horse still nursing its mother.

Suitable for mating — indicates a mare that has normal reproductive organs; in stallions, indicates fertility.

Teasing — using a male horse to approach a mare to determine her receptivity to breeding.

Thoroughbred — a breed of horse used mainly for flat and steeplechase racing.

Toe in — describes a horse whose pasterns and hooves deviate to the inside of an ideal midline when looking at a horse head-on; also called pigeon-toed.

Toe out — describes a horse whose pasterns and hooves deviate to the outside of an ideal midline when looking at a horse head-on.

Turf — a grass racing surface; also, when capitalized, a term referring to the sport of horse racing.

Resources and Recommended Reading

Books

The Blood-Horse Authoritative Guide to Auctions. Lexington, Ky.: Eclipse Press, 2004.

Bowen, Edward L. *Dynasties: Great Thoroughbred Stallions*. Lexington, Ky.: Eclipse Press, 2000.

Bowen, Edward L. *Matriarchs: Great Mares of the 20th Century*. Lexington, Ky.: Eclipse Press, 1999.

Faversham, Rommy and Leon Rasmussen, *Inbreeding to Superior Females*. Sydney, Australia: The Australian Bloodhorse Review, 1999. (Out of Print)

Hewitt, Abram S. *Sire Lines* (updated edition). Lexington, Ky.: Eclipse Press, 2006.

Hunter, Avalyn. *American Classic Pedigrees*. Lexington, Ky.: Eclipse Press, 2003.

Kirkpatrick, Arnold. *Investing in Thoroughbreds*. Lexington, Ky.: Eclipse Press, 2001.

Loving, Nancy, DVM. *Conformation and Performance*. Ossining, N.Y.: Breakthrough Publishers, 1997.

McLean, Ken. *Designing Speed in the Racehorse*. Neenah, Wisc.: Russell Meerdink Co., 2006.

McLean, Ken. *Genetic Heritage*. Lexington, Ky.: K & C McLean, 1996. (Out of Print)

McLean, Ken. *Quest for a Classic Winner: Pedigree Patterns of a Racehorse*. Neenah, Wisc.: Russell Meerdink Co., 2000.

Mitchell, Frank, Ph.D. *Racehorse Breeding Theories*. Neenah, Wisc.: Russell Meerdink Co., 2004.

Oliver, Robert and Bob Langrish. *A Photographic Guide to Conformation*. North Pomfret, Vt.: Trafalgar Square, 2003.

Porter, Alan. *Patterns of Greatness I*. London, England: Highflyer International, 1992.

Porter, Alan and Anne Peters. *Patterns of Greatness II: The Americans*. London, England: Highflyer International, 1995.

Proctor, Laura, ed. *New Thoroughbred Owners Handbook*. Lexington, Ky.: TOBA/Eclipse Press, 2003.

Tesio, Federico. *Tesio: In His Own Words*. Neenah, Wisc.: Russell Meerdink Co., 2005.

Thomas, Heather Smith. *The Horse Conformation Handbook*. North Adams, Mass.: Storey Publishing, 2005.

Toby, Milton C. and Karen L. Perch, Ph.D. *Understanding*

Business Basics. Lexington, Ky.: Eclipse Press, 2001.

Toby, Milton C. and Karen L. Perch, Ph.D. *Understanding Equine Law*. Lexington, Ky.: Eclipse Press, 1999.

Magazines and Supplements

The Blood-Horse magazine
The Blood-Horse *Source*
The Blood-Horse *Stallion Register*
The Blood-Horse *Auctions*
The Blood-Horse *Nicks*
The Blood-Horse *Sires*
The Blood-Horse *Dams*
TBH MarketWatch
Owner-Breeder International

Online Resources

The Blood-Horse
www.bloodhorse.com

Keeneland
www.keeneland.com

Fasig-Tipton Company
www.fasigtipton.com

Bloodstock Research Information Services
www.brisnet.com

Thoroughbred Owners and Breeders Association
www.toba.org

The Jockey Club
www.jockeyclub.com

The Jockey Club Equine Line
www.equineline.com

The Jockey Club Registry
registry.jockeyclub.com

The Greatest Game
www.thegreatestgame.com

Thoroughbred Heritage
www.thoroughbredheritage.com

Thoroughbred Pedigree Query
www.pedigreequery.com

Dosage: Pedigree and Performance
www.chef-de-race.com

American Association of Equine Practitioners
www.aaep.org

Equix Biomechanics
www.equixbio.com

Videos

Conformation: How to Buy a Winner. The Blood-Horse, 1998.

Insider's Guide to Buying Thoroughbreds at Auction. The Blood-Horse, 1999.

Software/CD-ROM Resources

Tesio Power pedigree software
www.tesiopower.com

Pedigree Planner pedigree software
www.pedigreeplanner.co.nz

American Produce Records (CD-ROM)
www.brisnet.com

Contributors

Rena Baer is assistant editor for Eclipse Press, the book division of Blood-Horse Publications. She lives in Lexington, Kentucky.

Bettina Cohen is a freelance writer who has been published in *The Blood-Horse* magazine among other publications. She lives in San Francisco.

Jacqueline Duke is editor of Eclipse Press, the book division of Blood-Horse Publications. She lives in Lexington, Kentucky.

Tom Hall is senior editor for Eclipse Press, the book division of Blood-Horse Publications. He lives in Lexington, Kentucky.

Judy L. Marchman is managing editor for Eclipse Press, the book division of Blood-Horse Publications. She lives in Lexington, Kentucky.

Eric Mitchell is research director of *The Blood-Horse* magazine and editor of *The Blood-Horse MarketWatch*, an industry newsletter. He lives in Lexington, Kentucky.

Les Sellnow is a horseman and equine journalist who writes regularly for *The Horse: Your Guide to Equine Health Care*. He also is the author of *Happy Trails: Your Complete Guide to Fun and Safe Trail Riding*. He lives in Riverton, Wyoming.